Language, Meaning and Context

John Lyons has been Professor of Linguistics at the University of Sussex since 1976. Born in Manchester in 1932 and educated at St Bede's College, Manchester, and Christ's College, Cambridge, he lectured at the School of Oriental and African Studies in London from 1957 to 1961 and at Cambridge from 1961 until 1964, when he became Professor of General Linguistics at Edinburgh University.

A frequent contributor to such publications as the *Journal of Linguistics* and the *Times Literary Supplement*, his own books include *Structural Semantics* (1963), *Theoretical Linguistics* (1968), *New Horizons in Linguistics* (1970) and the two-volume work, *Semantics* (1977). He is also the author of *Chomsky* (revised edition: 1977) in Fontana's Modern Masters series.

Fontana Linguistics

Published

Language Change: Progress or Decay?   Jean Aitchison

Understanding and Producing Speech
    Edward Matthei and Thomas Roeper

Forthcoming

Linguistics Today   Keith Brown

Language and Society   William Downes

JOHN LYONS

Language,
Meaning
and Context

Fontana Paperbacks

First published by Fontana Paperbacks 1981
Copyright © John Lyons 1981
Second impression October 1983
Third impression July 1986

Set in Monophoto Times

Made and printed in Great Britain by
Richard Clay (The Chaucer Press) Ltd,
Bungay, Suffolk

Contents

Part 4 Beyond the Sentence: Utterances and Texts

Introduction to Fontana Linguistics

In the past twenty-five years, linguistics – the systematic study of language – has come of age. It is a fast expanding and increasingly popular subject, which is now offered as a degree course at a number of universities. As a result of this expansion, psychologists, sociologists, philosophers, anthropologists, teachers, speech therapists and numerous others have realized that language is of crucial importance in their life and work. But when they tried to find out more about the subject, a major problem faced them – the technical and often narrow nature of much writing about linguistics.

The Fontana Linguistics series is an attempt to solve this problem by presenting current findings in a lucid and non-technical way. Its object is twofold. First, it hopes to outline the 'state of play' in certain crucial areas of the subject, concentrating on what is happening now, rather than on surveying the past. Secondly, it aims to show how linguistics links up with other disciplines such as sociology, psychology, philosophy, speech therapy and language teaching.

The series will, we hope, give readers a fuller understanding of the relationship between language and other aspects of human behaviour, as well as equipping those who wish to find out more about the subject with a basis from which to read some of the more technical literature in textbooks and journals.

Jean Aitchison
London School of Economics

Preface

When I was asked to contribute a short book on semantics to this series, I thought that I would merely need to abridge and simplify particular sections of my two-volume *Semantics* (1977). In the event, it seemed preferable to write to a quite different plan. Since all books have a will of their own, which does not always submit to that of their authors, *Language, Meaning and Context* differs considerably from *Semantics* not only in length, style and level of exposition, but also in emphasis. Nevertheless, I have endeavoured to make the two works notationally and terminologically compatible with one another, and also with my recent introductory textbook *Language and Linguistics* (1981).

I take a very broad view of semantics: for me, semantics is by definition the study of meaning, and linguistic semantics is the study of all the different kinds of meaning that are systematically encoded in natural languages. It follows that I include within linguistic semantics a good deal of what many of my colleagues would classify as pragmatics. But I do draw a distinction between competence and performance, on the one hand, and between meaning and use, on the other. Furthermore, contrary to the impression gained by several reviewers of *Semantics*, I am far from being hostile to formal semantics. Indeed, one of my principal aims in writing this book has been to show how formal semantics, conceived as the analysis of a central part of the meaning of sentences – their propositional content – can be integrated, in principle if not yet in practice, within the broader field of linguistic semantics. I have also had the complementary purpose of showing that formal, truth-conditional, semantics, as currently practised, fails to handle other kinds of linguistic meaning.

I should like to put on record my indebtedness to Jean Aitchison for her invaluable editorial advice and assistance. It was she who invited me to write the book and suggested a general plan, and she has done much, through her comments on the first draft, to improve the text and make it more readable. She has also supplied me with several of the more felicitous chapter-headings and quotations. Needless to say, I take full responsibility for the errors and misplaced pedantry that she has failed to persuade me to remove.

John Lyons
University of Sussex

PART 1

Introduction

1 *Setting the Scene*

Introductory comments

'Hell's bells. Don't you understand English? When I say to you, "Tell me what you mean," you can only reply, "I would wish to say so and so." "Never mind what you wish to say," I reply. "Tell me what you mean." '

Tom Stoppard, *Professional Foul*

The verb 'mean' and the noun 'meaning', like many other English words, are used in a wide range of contexts and with several different meanings. For example, to take the case of the verb: as used in *Mary means well* it implies that Mary intends no harm. This notion of intention would normally be lacking in *That red flag means danger*. In saying this, one would not be suggesting that the flag had plans to endanger anyone; one would be drawing attention to the fact that a red flag is conventionally employed to indicate that there is some peril in the surrounding environment, such as a crevasse on a snowy hillside. Similar to the red flag use of 'mean', in one respect at least, is its use in *Smoke means fire*. In both cases one thing is said to be a *sign* of something else: from the presence of the sign, a red flag or smoke, anyone with the requisite knowledge can infer the existence of what it signifies, danger or fire. But there is an important difference. Whereas smoke is a *natural* sign of fire, causally connected with what it signifies, the red flag is a *conventional* sign of danger: it is a culturally established *symbol*. These distinctions between the intentional and the nonintentional, on the one hand, and between what is natural and what is conventional, or symbolic, on the other, play a central part in the theoretical investigation of meaning.

That the verb 'mean' is being employed in different

senses in the examples that I have used so far is evident from the fact that *Mary means trouble* is ambiguous: it can be taken like *Mary means well* or like *Smoke means fire*. Indeed, with a little imagination it is possible to devise a context, or scenario, in which the verb 'mean' in *Mary means trouble* can be plausibly interpreted in the way that it would normally be interpreted in *That red flag means danger*. Most language-utterances, we shall see, depend for their interpretation upon the context in which they are used. And the vast majority of them have a wider range of meanings than first come to mind. Utterances containing the word 'meaning' (or the verb 'mean') are no different from other English utterances in this respect.

Let us now take yet another use of the verb 'mean'. If I say *'Soporific' means "tending to produce sleep"*, I am obviously not imputing intentionality to the English word 'soporific'. It might be argued, however, that there is an essential, though indirect, connection between what a person mean, or intends, and what the words that he uses are conventionally held to mean. This point has been much discussed by philosophers of language. I will not pursue it here. Nor will I take up the related point, that there is also an intrinsic, and possibly more direct, connection between what a person means and what he means to say. (This point is relevant to our understanding of the Tom Stoppard quotation at the beginning of this chapter.) On the other hand, later in this book I will be drawing upon a particular version of the distinction between saying what one means and meaning what one says – another distinction that has been extensively discussed in the philosophy of language. Intentionality is certainly of importance in any theoretical account that we might give of the meaning of language-utterances, even if it is not a property of the words of which these utterances are composed. For the moment, let us simply note that it is the meaning of the word 'mean' as it is employed in *'Soporific' means "tending to produce sleep"* that is of central concern to the linguist.

One could go on for a long time enumerating and discussing examples of the multifarious uses of the words 'mean' and 'meaning'. One could also note and discuss utterances in which several uses are combined or one meaning of these words shades into another. This phenomenon is cleverly exploited in the advertising slogan *Beanz meanz Heinz*. This slogan derives a good deal of its effect, of course, from its violation of one of the grammatical rules of Standard English, its staccato, monosyllabic rhythm and partial rhymes, and its neat spelling pun. But it also trades successfully, as many advertisements do, upon the possibility of blending two or three normally distinct senses of a word in such a way that the reader or hearer is hard put to assign a single determinate interpretation to it.

The main point that I want to make in this section is, not so much that the words 'mean' and 'meaning' themselves have many meanings, but rather that these several meanings are interconnected, and shade into one another, in various ways. This is why the topic of *meaning* is of concern to so many of the social sciences and does not fall wholly within any single one of them. Psychologists might want to know the meaning of some abnormality of behaviour; anthropologists might be seeking the meaning of primitive religious rituals; ethologists might be researching into the meaning of behaviour patterns in animals, and so on.

Of all the disciplines with an interest in meaning, *linguistics* – the scientific study of language – is perhaps the one to which it is of greatest concern. Meaningfulness is essential to languages as we know them; and it is arguable that the very notion of a language without meaning is logically incoherent. Moreover, although many kinds of behaviour can be described as meaningful, the range, diversity and complexity of meaning expressed in language is unmatched in any other human or non-human communicative behaviour.

Part of the difference between language and other kinds

of communicative behaviour derives from intentionality and conventionality, referred to earlier. An animal normally expresses its feelings or attitudes by means of behaviour which is arguably non-intentional and non-conventional. For example, a crab will signal aggression by waving a large claw. A human being, on the other hand, will only rarely express his anger, whether intentionally or not, by shaking his fist. More often, he will convey feelings such as aggression by means of language-utterances like *You'll be sorry for this* or *I'll sue you* or *How dare you behave like that!* As far as the words he uses are concerned, it is clear that there is no natural, non-conventional, link between their form and their meaning. But, as we shall see throughout this book, there is much more to accounting for the meaningfulness of language than simply saying what each word means.

How, then, do linguists cope with the meaning of language-utterances? As with other disciplines in general and the social sciences in particular, their ways of dealing with any part of their subject-matter vary in accordance with the prevailing intellectual climate. Indeed, there have been times in the recent past, notably in America in the period between 1930 and the end of the 1950s, when *linguistic semantics* – the study of meaning in language – was very largely neglected. This was because meaning was felt to be inherently subjective and, at least temporarily, beyond the scope of scientific investigation. A more particular reason for this comparative neglect of linguistic semantics was the influence of behaviourist psychology upon some, though not all, schools of American linguistics. Largely as a result of the rise of Chomsky's theory of generative grammar, the influence of behaviourism is no longer as strong as it was even twenty years ago; and not only linguists, but also psychologists, are prepared to admit as data much that was previously rejected as subjective and unreliable. For other reasons too, having to do with the technical advances made in linguistics, on the one hand, and in logic and the philosophy of language, on the other, linguistic semantics is currently enjoying a very considerable revival of interest.

This book, therefore, examines the strengths and weaknesses of the most important notions of linguistic semantics which have arisen out of contact with philosophers in recent years. The treatment is, of necessity, selective; it is also somewhat personal, in that I have relied upon my own judgment, rather than upon the consensus of my colleagues, in the determination of what I should include and what I should exclude or merely mention without detailed discussion. The arguments, even at the level at which they are presented here, are inevitably rather technical in places; and there is a certain amount of specialized terminology to be mastered. One cannot talk about language with any degree of precision without making use of a fairly formal framework. However, it is my belief that there is nothing in what follows that is too technical for the seriously intentioned non-linguist. And it is my hope that those who read the book in its entirety will not only have acquired an outline grasp of some of the ways in which linguists have approached the problem of meaning in the last quarter-century, but will also have developed the ability to read other works in the field with a critical appreciation of their qualities and their limitations.

Assumptions and definitions

In a book of this kind, we have to make a certain number of assumptions, if only to get started. Since we shall be concerned almost exclusively with language, I will begin by assuming that everyone knows, in a general sort of way at least, what a language is and how it is used. I will also assume that all languages have words and sentences; that both words and sentences are meaningful; that the meaning of a sentence depends, in part, upon the meaning of the words of which it is composed; and that everyone reading this book can identify and interpret the words and sentences of any language, including English, in which he or she is competent. Actually, these assumptions are far from being as innocent as they might appear at first sight. Some of them will need to be looked at more carefully later. But we can make a fair amount of progress without questioning them and can now turn to one of the main topics of this chapter – how to talk about language.

Languages can be used to talk not only about the world in general, but also about themselves and other languages. Since this latter function is rather special, it is customary nowadays to identify it by means of a distinctive technical term: *metalinguistic*. As we shall see in a later chapter, linguists and logicians have constructed various highly formalized *metalanguages*, whose sole function it is to describe ordinary, natural languages as precisely as possible. Throughout this book we shall be using English as our principal metalanguage. It will be helpful, however, if we furnish ourselves with a number of notational and terminological conventions, so that, as far as possible, we know what we are talking about when English, or any other natural language, is being used metalinguistically. There are certain rules that we all follow, without normally being conscious of them, in the everyday metalinguistic use of our native language. But they cannot, unfortunately, prevent misunderstanding in all contexts, especially when a written language is used to refer to a spoken language.

Words, as we said earlier, have meaning. They also have a form: in fact, in English and any other language for which a writing-system has been devised and is in common use, they have both a written and a spoken form. We shall not generally need to draw a distinction between written and spoken forms. But it will certainly be necessary to distinguish the word itself from both its form and its meaning. We can use the ordinary written form of a word to stand, not only for the word itself as a composite unit with both form and meaning, but also for either the form or the meaning considered independently of one another. This is what is done in the everyday metalinguistic use of English and other languages. However, in order to make it clear which of these three different metalinguistic functions a form is fulfilling on a particular occasion we need to establish distinctive notational conventions.

Regrettably, there are no generally accepted conventions; and the most commonly used systems fail to draw even the minimal, and rather obvious, distinctions introduced so far. In the present work, single quotation-marks will be employed for words, and for other expressions with both form and meaning; italics (without quotation-marks) for forms; and double quotation-marks for meanings. Subscript numerals will be added, on occasion, to distinguish one homonym from another – homonyms being different words with the same form. For example, 'bank$_1$', and 'bank$_2$' are homonyms: they share the form *bank*, but they differ in their meaning, 'bank$_1$' having the meaning "financial institution" and 'bank$_2$' having the meaning "sloping side of a river" (see Fig. 1). Homonymy is not

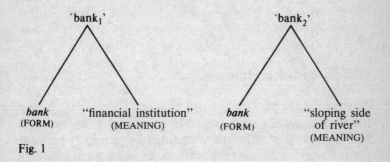

Fig. 1

quite as straightforward as has been implied here. It will be discussed in some detail in a later chapter. So too will the differences among the various senses in which the term 'word' is used both technically and in everyday discourse. Until then, 'word' will be employed rather uncritically.

A moment's reflection will show that all we have done so far is to systematize and codify, for our own special purposes, one part of the ordinary metalinguistic use of English. When the man in the street wants to refer to a word, he does so by *citing* it in either its written or spoken form. For example, he might say

Can you tell me what 'synonymy' means?

And one possible response would be

I'm sorry I can't: look it up in the dictionary,

where 'it', in context, both refers to and can be replaced by 'synonymy'. Similarly, standard dictionaries identify words by means of their form, listing them according to a purely conventional ordering of the letters of the alphabet, which we have all learned for this very purpose at school. Also, most dictionaries distinguish homonyms, as we have done with 'bank₁' and 'bank₂', by assigning distinctive numbers to them and giving a separate entry to each.

Words: forms and meanings

But the majority of English words have more than one form associated with them. For example, both 'bank₁', and 'bank₂' share the singular form *bank* and the plural form *banks* (not to mention the possessive forms, *bank's* and *banks'*, which differ from *banks* in written, though not in spoken English); 'sing' has the grammatically distinct forms *sing*, *sings*, *singing*, *sang* and *sung*; and so on. However, in each case, one of the forms of a word is conventionally accepted as its *citation-form*: i.e., as the form that is used to refer to the word as a whole. And this is the form that appears, alphabetized, at the head of each entry in a standard dictionary. It is worth noting that the citation-form of a word is not necessarily the form of the word that a grammarian might identify as its root or stem. Generally speaking, in English the citation-form of a word is identical with its stem-form. But this is not so in all languages. Throughout this book, we shall use whatever citation-form is most generally accepted in the lexicographical tradition of the languages being referred to.

Not only do most English words have more than one form. They may also have more than one meaning; and in this respect English is typical of all natural languages. For example, what we have identified as 'bank$_1$' has other meanings in addition to "financial institution", including "store, or storage place" (cf. 'data bank', 'blood bank' etc.), "funds held by the dealer in certain gambling games". Once again, we can arbitrarily assign numbers to the several meanings of a word in order to distinguish them symbolically one from another as follows. Given that X is the citation-form of a word, we refer to that word as 'X' and distinguish its several meanings as "X_a" "X_b" "X_c", etc. To return to the 'bank$_1$' example, we could regard "financial institution" as meaning$_a$, "store or storage place" as meaning$_b$, and so on. Of course this is simply a convenient notational device, which presupposes two things: first, that the meanings of words are separate from each other; second, that we can distinguish one meaning from another. Our notational device is based, then, on the assumption that word-meanings are both discrete and distinguishable – an assumption made in standard dictionaries, and one which, for the time being at least, we shall not challenge.

But it is a salutary experience for anyone who has not previously done this to take a set of common English words – e.g., 'bank$_1$', 'bank$_2$' (and perhaps also 'bank$_3$', meaning "row of oars, dials, typewriter-keys, etc."), 'game', 'table', 'tree' – and to look them up in half-a-dozen comprehensive and authoritative dictionaries. He will find many differences of detail, not only in the definitions that are offered, but also in the number of meanings that are recognized for each word. He will also find that some dictionaries, but not all, operate with a further level of differentiation, such that, not only is "X_1" distinguished from "X_2", "X_3", etc., but "X_{1a}" is distinguished from "X_{1b}", "X_{1c}", etc.; and so on. For example, "funds held by the dealer" and "person holding such funds" might be regarded as two sub-meanings of 'bank$_1$'. At the very least, the experience of comparing a number of different dictionaries in this way should have the effect of making it clear that it is not as easy to say how many meanings a word has as casual reflection might suggest.

At this point a further question arises which needs to be put on the agenda. If homonyms are words which have the same form but differ in meaning, why do we say that, for example, "financial institution" and "store, or storage place" are two different meanings of the same word? Should one not say as we did for 'bank$_1$' and 'bank$_2$' that two different words are involved? Some theoreticians have taken the view that one should do just this whenever a difference of meaning can be established. It is easy to see that this view simply transfers the practical problem of deciding how many different meanings a word has to a different level in the organization of the dictionary.

There are two reasons why 'bank$_1$' and 'bank$_2$' are traditionally regarded as homonyms. First of all, they differ etymologically: 'bank$_1$' was borrowed from Italian (cf. 'banca') in the fifteenth century; 'bank$_2$' can be traced back through Middle English, and beyond, to a Scandinavian word (related ultimately to the German source of the Italian 'banca', but, differing from it in its historical development). Second, the meanings of 'bank$_1$', on the other hand, are interrelated in various ways; and the order in which they are numbered and listed in the dictionary will generally reflect the editor's view of how closely one meaning is related, either historically or logically, to its neighbours. We shall be looking more closely later at the notion of relatedness of meaning. For the moment, it is sufficient to note that we can usually identify one meaning of a word as being more central than the others. This is the meaning that I expect the reader to have in mind whenever I refer, without further qualification, to the meaning of a word by means of the symbolic device of double quotation-marks introduced above.

Sentences and utterances

One of our initial assumptions, it will be recalled, was that the meaning of a sentence depends, in part, upon the meaning of the words of which it is composed. The other factor, quite clearly, is the grammatical structure of the sentence. For two sentences can be composed of exactly the same words (each word being interpreted in the same way) and yet differ in meaning. This is exemplified by

'It was raining yesterday'

and

'Was it raining yesterday?'

Or again, and somewhat differently, by

'John admires Mary'

and

'Mary admires John'.

It will be noted that I am using single quotation-marks for sentences, as well as for words and other expressions with form and meaning.

Until recently, linguists have been more concerned with describing the meaning of individual words than with specifying in detail how the meaning of the sentence is derived from the meaning of its constituent words by means of rules which make reference to its grammatical structure. But the situation has changed dramatically in the last fifteen years or so. For simplicity of exposition, we shall make the distinction between word-meaning and sentence-meaning one of the main organizing principles of this book, dealing with the former in Part 2 and the latter in Part 3. It must be emphasized, however, that this method of organizing the material carries with it no implication whatsoever about the logical priority of word-meaning over sentence-meaning, or vice versa. There is no point in discussing the question of logical priority until we have built up rather more of the theoretical framework.

The distinction between sentence-meaning and the meaning of utterances and texts provides us with a further organizing principle. This distinction cannot be taken for granted in the way that the one between word-meaning and sentence-meaning can. Not only is it less familiar to laymen. It is also the subject of a good deal of controversy, not to say confusion, among specialists. Most of the detail may be left for Part 4. But a few general points must be made here.

In everyday English, 'utterance' usually refers to the spoken language, and 'text' to the written. Throughout this book, both words will be extended, so that each denotes stretches of either speech or writing. It will be assumed that speech is prior to writing, not only historically, but also – subject to one or two important qualifications – in respect of its structure and function. Usually therefore we shall cast our generalizations about language in terms which make them more appropriate to speaking than they may be, in certain instances, to writing. For example, we shall talk about the person producing an utterance as the speaker and about the person for whom it is intended as the hearer. But language is not speech. Indeed, one of the most striking properties of natural languages is their relative independence of the *medium* in which they are manifest. Language is still language, whether it manifests itself as speech or writing and, if written, regardless of whether it is written in the normal alphabet or in braille, morse-code etc. The degree of correspondence between written and spoken language varies somewhat, for historical and cultural reasons, from one language to another. But in English, and in most of the languages likely to be familiar to readers of this book, most sentences of the spoken language can be put into correspondence with written sentences. The fact that this is not a one-to-one correspondence will occupy us later. For the present, it should be noted that 'utterance', like 'text', is to be interpreted as covering stretches of either written or spoken language, or both, according to context.

Nothing further needs to be said, at this point, about texts. Actually, I shall have nothing to say about texts until we get to Chapter 9. In the meantime we can think of texts as sequences of utterances. But the term 'utterance' is sometimes ambiguous in a way that 'text' is not. In one sense, it denotes a particular kind of behaviour. In its other relevant sense, it denotes, not the behaviour itself, but the products of that behaviour: not speaking (or writing), but what is spoken (or written). Very often authors use the term without making it clear in what sense it is to be taken. Sometimes they define it in one sense and then use it in another; or, worse still, switch randomly between one and the other. Obviously, the two senses are related; but the nature of the relation is not self-evident, and it will be discussed in Part 4.

Meanwhile, we will establish the terminological convention that, whenever the term 'utterance' is used in this book without further qualification, it is to be interpreted in the second of the two senses identified above: that is, as denoting the products of a particular kind of behaviour. Utterances, in this sense of the term, are what some philosophers of language call *inscriptions*: i.e., sequences of symbols in some physical medium. For example, a spoken utterance is normally inscribed (in this technical sense of 'inscribe') in the medium of sound; a written utterance is inscribed in some other suitable medium which makes it visually identifiable. Furthermore, insofar as languages are used, typically if not necessarily, for communication, utterances can be regarded as signals which are transmitted from a sender to a receiver along some appropriate channel. Utterance-inscriptions will be distinguished notationally from sentences by using italics.

Natural-language utterances, it must be emphasized, are not just sequences or *strings* of word-forms. Superimposed upon the verbal component of any spoken utterance, there is always and necessarily a non-verbal component, which linguists further subdivide into a *prosodic* sub-component and *paralinguistic* sub-component. Just where the line should be drawn between these two sub-components need not concern us here. Let us merely note that the prosodic contour of an utterance includes its intonation, and perhaps also its stress-pattern; and that paralinguistic features include such things as tone of voice, loudness, rhythm, tempo, etc. These non-verbal features of an utterance are just as relevant to the determination of its meaning as word-meaning and grammatical meaning – both of which are encoded in the verbal component. Only the verbal component is *medium-transferable*: that is, its structure can, in principle, be held constant under the conversion of speech to writing. Some writing-systems do include more or less conventionalized principles for the punctuation of written utterances. But these never match significant differences of intonation in the spoken language. Even when the normal conventions of punctuation are supplemented with such typographical devices as the use of capitals, italics, bold print, accent-marks etc., there may be some part of the prosodic contour of an utterance that is left unrepresented.

This is an important point. All linguists and most philosophers pay at least lip-service to the principle of the priority of spoken language. But they, no less than others, have to be very careful if they want to take full account of this principle in the construction of a satisfactory theory of linguistic semantics. The habits and prejudices of literacy are all-pervasive in our everyday thinking about language. And many of these have been carried over uncritically into theoretical accounts of meaning and communication. I cannot go into this question in detail. However, it must by now be clear that there are problems associated with the medium-transferability of language in respect of both the paralinguistic and the prosodic part of the non-verbal component of utterances. One of the practical consequences of this fact is that almost every written utterance cited in this, and other, books on language can be put into correspondence with significantly different spoken utterances. The written utterance *Mary won't come*, for example, can be pronounced, or read aloud, in several ways, indicative of boredom, surprise or certainty. I shall try to choose my examples so that, with sufficient explanation at the time, it does not matter, for the particular issue that is under discussion, which of several significantly different spoken utterances is chosen by the reader. But I may not always succeed. When one is writing, it is especially difficult not to fall victim to the habits, if not to the prejudices, of literacy.

I am taking for granted, for the time being, the reader's ability to identify the sentences of any language in which he is competent. I will now make the further assumption that some utterances, actual or potential, are sentences, whereas others are not. Some utterances are non-sentences because they are grammatically incorrect; others, because they are grammatically incomplete. On the other hand, there are sentences which, though fully grammatical, are in one way or another unacceptable: that is, unutterable in all normal contexts other than those involving metalinguistic reference to them. For example, there might be a taboo, in a certain society, upon the use of the verb 'die', rather than 'pass away', with expressions referring to members of the speaker's or hearer's immediate family. Thus, the sentence
      'His father died last night',
but not the equally grammatical
      'My father died last night',
might be acceptable. Or again, it might be unacceptable for a social inferior to address a social superior with a second-person pronoun (meaning "you"). There are

many such culture-dependent dimensions of acceptability. Some of them, as we shall see later, are encoded in the grammar and vocabulary of particular languages.

Somewhat different are those dimensions of acceptability which have to do with rationality and logical coherence. For example,

'I believe that it happened because it is impossible' might be regarded as unacceptable from this point of view – though it is paradoxical, rather than meaningless or contradictory. What makes the above sentence unacceptable, in most contexts, is the fact that in uttering it the speaker appears to be calling attention to his own irrationality; and this is an odd thing to do in most normal circumstances. However, even such utterances may be fully acceptable in certain contexts. It is worth bearing in mind that the acceptability of grammatical and meaningful sentences is not something that can be decided independently of the context in which they might or might not be uttered.

Throughout Parts 2 and 3 of this book we shall be restricting our attention to utterances that are also sentences. We shall leave for Part 4 the task of specifying in some detail what exactly is meant by the expression 'to utter a sentence' and explaining how it can be extended to cover grammatically correct, but incomplete, utterances, which constitute a particular subclass of non-sentences. Most of our everyday utterances may well fall into this subclass of non-sentences.

The difference between sentence-meaning and utterance-meaning will be dealt with, as I said, in Part 4. At this stage it will be sufficient to make two general points. First, sentence-meaning is (to a high degree) *context-independent*, whereas utterance-meaning is not. Second, there is an intrinsic connection between the meaning of a sentence and the *characteristic use*, not of the particular sentence as such, but of the whole class of sentences to which the sentence belongs by virtue of its grammatical structure. This connection is usually, and for the moment satisfactorily, formulated as follows: a declarative sentence is one that belongs, by virtue of its grammatical structure, to the class whose members are used, characteristically, to make statements, as in 'Guinness is good for you' or 'I prefer mine neat'; an interrogative sentence is one that is similarly related in terms of form and function, to questions, as in 'What time is lunch?'; and so on. When we said earlier of 'It was raining yesterday' and 'Was it raining yesterday?' that their meaning was determined, in part, by their grammatical structure, we were tacitly appealing to our knowledge of the characteristic use of declarative and interrogative sentences. It will be observed that the notion of characteristic use has been associated with classes of sentences, rather than with each and every member. This is important, even though some sentences are never used in normal circumstances with the function that characterizes the grammatically defined class to which they belong and, as we shall see later, all sentences can be used occasionally in the performance of so-called *indirect speech acts* (declarative sentences being used to ask questions, interrogative sentences to issue requests, etc.). However, it is obviously impossible that most declarative sentences should normally be used to ask questions, most interrogative sentences to make statements, and so on. For declarative and interrogative sentences are, by definition, sentences with the characteristic use that is here ascribed to them. Moreover, if a language does not have a grammatically defined class of sentences with one or other of these characteristic uses, then it does not have declarative or interrogative sentences, as the case may be.

Sentence-meaning, then, is related to utterance-meaning by virtue of the notion of characteristic use, but it differs from it by virtue of the fact that the meaning of a sentence is independent of the particular contexts in which it may be uttered. To determine the meaning of an utterance, on the other hand, we have to take contextual factors into account. Qualifications and modifications will need to be made later. But this will do for the purpose of organizing the content of the book between Parts 3 and 4.

I have been using the term 'semantics' in a comparatively broad sense without distinguishing it from 'pragmatics'. One of the ways of drawing this distinction is in terms of the distinction drawn here between sentence-meaning and utterance-meaning. Given this distinction, Part 3 can be seen as dealing with *semantics* and Part 4 with *pragmatics*. But there are many other ways of distinguishing semantics from pragmatics. For example, many linguists have subsumed semantics under *competence* (knowledge of the language) and pragmatics under *performance* (use of the language). There is nothing unreasonable about defining the field of semantics and pragmatics in this way. Indeed, on a broader, and more natural, interpretation of 'linguistic competence' than the one that is customarily adopted by generative grammarians, this way of distinguishing the two fields has much to recommend it. And it is not necessarily incompatible with definitions based on the distinction between sentence-meaning and utterance-meaning. As things stand, however, nothing but confusion results from the attempt to collapse two, or more, distinctions into one.

Various theories of meaning

So far, we have been talking in a preliminary way about word-meaning, sentence-meaning and utterance-meaning without making any attempt to say what meaning is. There are several distinguishable, and more or less well-known, theories of meaning. Among them, one might mention the following:

(i)   the *referential* theory ("the meaning of an expression is what it refers to, or stands for": e.g., 'Fido' means Fido, 'dog' means either the class of dogs or the property they all share);

(ii) the *ideational*, or *mentalistic*, theory ("the meaning of an expression is the idea, or concept, associated with it in the mind of anyone who knows it");

(iii) the *behaviourist* theory ("the meaning of an expression is either the stimulus that evokes it or the response that it evokes, or a combination of both, on particular occasions of utterance");

(iv) the *meaning-is-use* theory ("the meaning of an expression is determined by, if not identical with, its use in the language");

(v) the *verificationist* theory ("the meaning of an expression, if it has one, is determined by the verifiability of the sentences, or propositions, containing it");

(vi) the *truth-conditional* theory ("the meaning of an expression is its contribution to the truth-conditions of the sentences containing it").

None of these, in my view, is satisfactory as a comprehensive and empirically well-motivated theory of meaning in natural languages. But each of them has contributed in one way or another to the background assumptions of those who are currently working towards the construction of such a theory. I will not go into the details of any of the above-mentioned theories at this point. However, I will make reference to some of the key-concepts that distinguish them in the course of the chapters that follow, and I will explain them in the context in which they are invoked and applied. Limitations of space will prevent me from going fully into the historical connections among the several theories or the philosophical issues associated with them.

It is worth noting here, however, that one philosophically defensible response to the question "What is meaning?" is "There is no such thing". This was the response, for example, of the later Wittgenstein; and it has to be taken seriously. It clearly makes sense to enquire about the meaning of words, sentences and utterances, just as it makes sense to ask what they mean. In doing so, we are using the English words 'meaning' and 'mean' in one of their everyday metalinguistic functions. As we saw earlier, there are also other everyday meanings, or uses, of 'meaning' and 'mean'; and some philosophers at least have held these to be intimately connected with, and perhaps more basic than, the one that has just been exemplified. Interestingly enough they cannot always be matched one-to-one with the meanings, or uses, of otherwise comparable expressions in such familiar European languages as French, German, Italian, Russian or Spanish. This fact of itself is worth pondering. For the present, however, I am concerned to make the simple point that we cannot infer the existence of meanings, as physical or mental entities, from the existence and meaningfulness of the everyday English word 'meaning'.

It was part of Wittgenstein's purpose to emphasize the diversity of communicative functions fulfilled by language. His slogan 'Don't look for the meaning look for the use' (which does not necessarily lead to the meaning-is-use theory, though it is commonly so interpreted) must be understood with reference to this purpose. Like the so-called ordinary-language philosophers, such as J.L. Austin (whose theory of *speech acts* we shall be looking at in Part 4), he pointed out that the question "What is meaning?" tends to attract answers which are either so general as to be almost vacuous or so narrow in their definition of 'meaning' as to leave out of account most of what ordinary users of a language think is relevant when one puts to them more specific questions about the meaning of this or that expression in their language.

In what follows I shall take a fairly broad view of meaning. Furthermore, I will assume, without arguing for it at this stage, that there is an intrinsic connection between meaning and communication. This assumption is not uncontroversial, but it is one that is commonly made by philosophers, psychologists and linguists. It enables us to give a better account of the relation between form and meaning in natural languages than does any currently available alternative. And I would emphasize that, although I have referred here to various philosophical theories of meaning and shall draw freely upon them throughout, I am not concerned with philosophical issues as such, but with the theoretical and practical problems that arise in the description of natural languages. It is my belief, which I shall endeavour to justify as we go along, that much recent work in linguistic semantics and pragmatics is distorted, in certain important respects, by its failure to give full recognition to structural and functional differences among languages.

Descriptive and non-descriptive meaning

I will make no attempt to set forth at this point a comprehensive classification of the different kinds of meaning that a linguistically oriented theory of semantics and pragmatics should cover. It seems preferable to introduce the relevant technical concepts gradually and in relation to actual data. However, it might be helpful to draw even now one very broad distinction which can be developed in more detail later.

This is the distinction between *descriptive* (or *propositional*) and *non-descriptive* (or *non-propositional*) meaning. (Alternative terms, more or less equivalent with 'descriptive', are 'cognitive' and 'referential'.) With regard to descriptive meaning, it is a universally acknowledged fact that languages can be used to make descriptive statements, which are true or false according to whether the *propositions* that they express are true or false. This fact is given particular prominence in the truth-conditional theory of semantics, which has been extremely important in recent years.

Non-descriptive meaning is more heterogeneous and, in the view of many philosophers and linguists, less central. It includes what I will refer to as an *expressive* component. (Alternative more or less equivalent terms are 'affective', 'attitudinal' and 'emotive'.) Expressive meaning – i.e., the kind of meaning by virtue of which a speaker expresses, rather than describes, his beliefs, attitudes and feelings – is often held to fall within the scope of stylistics or pragmatics. It will be demonstrated that some kinds of expressive meaning are unquestionably a part of sentence-meaning. It follows from this fact that, for anyone who draws the distinction between semantics and pragmatics in terms of the distinction between sentences and utterances, expressive meaning falls, at least in part, within semantics. Interestingly enough, languages seem to vary considerably in the degree to which they grammaticalize expressive meaning. English does so to a relatively low degree. Like all natural languages, however, it encodes expressive meaning in much of its vocabulary and in the prosodic structure of utterances. It is arguable that the meaning of sentences is independent of the prosodic contour with which they are uttered (though most linguists do not take this view); and perhaps also of exclamatory and contextualizing particles of the kind that one finds in many languages. But expressive meaning is also combined with descriptive meaning, as we shall see, in many ordinary nouns, verbs and adjectives.

Other kinds of non-propositional meaning may be left until later. It is worth emphasizing, however, that the expressive functions of language cannot be sharply differentiated from their social and instrumental functions. We are social beings with socially prescribed and socially sanctioned purposes. We may not always be consciously projecting one kind of self-image rather than another; we may not be deliberately expressing the feelings and attitudes that we do express in order to manipulate the hearer and achieve one goal rather than another. Nevertheless, it is impossible to express our feelings, attitudes and beliefs by means of language, however personal and spontaneous they might be, otherwise than in terms of the distinctions that are encoded in particular language-systems. As we shall see throughout this book, but more especially in Part 4, expressive meaning necessarily merges with what many authors have referred to as *interpersonal*, or *social-conative*, meaning. Unless this is appreciated, it would seem to be impossible to give a proper semantic account of even such common, though not universal, grammatical categories as tense and mood.

Summary

In this chapter, I have, first of all, set up some notational conventions for dealing with meaning. Second, I have introduced a number of matters which will be explored more fully later in the book, in particular word-meaning (Part 2), sentence-meaning (Part 3) and utterance-meaning (Part 4). Third, I have listed a number of theories of meaning which have influenced its study in recent years, and have drawn a broad distinction between descriptive (propositional) meaning, and non-descriptive (non-propositional) meaning. We can now go on to the next stage, a consideration of words and phrases.

Words and Phrases

2 Working with Words

Words as meaningful units

'Before considering the meaning of words, let us examine them first as occurrences in the sensible world.'
Bertrand Russell, *An Inquiry into Meaning and Truth*

The chapter from which I have taken the above quotation bears the title 'What is a word?'. The answer that Russell gave to this question differs in several respects from the answer that most linguists and philosophers would give nowadays. Apart from anything else, modern conceptions of the phonological structure of languages have invalidated the view that words, considered as "occurrences in the sensible world", are purely physical entities, as Russell held them to be. Also, it is not always as easy to say that something is or is not a word as he, like most non-linguists, was inclined to suppose. Nevertheless, it is still possible to treat words, as Russell did, from two points of view: on the one hand as forms and on the other as what I will call expressions. As we shall see, the term 'word', in everyday usage, is ambiguous with respect to this distinction. When we look at words as meaningful units we also have to cope with the fact that one form may be associated with several meanings (homonymy and polysemy) and that the same meaning can be associated with different forms (synonymy). These topics will be the concern of this chapter.

Forms and expressions

'. . . . the meaning of a sentence depends, in part, upon the meaning of the words of which it is composed.' This is one of the several innocent-looking assumptions, listed early in the preceding chapter, which I said would need to be looked at more carefully. I now wish to take up in more detail the status of words as meaningful units. In what sense of 'word' is it true to say that sentences are composed of words?

There are, in fact, two quite different distinctions to be taken into account, and it is important not to confuse the one with the other. The first is what the American philosopher C.S. Peirce referred to as the distinction between words as *tokens* and words as *types* (in a specialized, but now quite common, sense of these two terms). This is readily explained by means of a simple example. Consider the following sentence:

'He who laughs last laughs longest'.

From one point of view, it can be said to contain six words: it is six words long. From another point of view, however, it can be said to contain only five words, since two of the words – the third and the fifth (*laughs*) – are identical: they are different tokens of the same type. Put like this, the notion of type/token identity is not difficult to grasp. And, generally speaking, it is clear enough in everyday life when the term 'word' is to be understood in one sense rather than the other with respect to Peirce's distinction.

There is, however, a second distinction which is also relevant at this point; and this too may be explained by means of a simple example. How many words are there in the following sentence:

'If he is right and I am wrong, we are both in trouble'?

Once again, there are two correct answers to the question. But the fact this is so has nothing to do with the difference between types and tokens. It rests upon the difference between words as *forms* and words as *expressions*. There are thirteen forms in the sentence in question, and each of them represents (or instantiates) a different type. From this point of view, therefore, they are different words. From another point of view, however, three of the words – *is*, *am* and *are* – can be described as different forms of the same word. In one sense of 'word', our sentence is composed of thirteen words; in another, equally common and equally correct, sense of the term, it is composed of only eleven words. Let us express this difference in the meaning of 'word' by saying that the sentence is composed of thirteen *word-forms* and eleven *word-expressions*. It is word-expressions, not word-forms, that are listed in a conventional dictionary. And they are listed, as we saw in Chapter 1, according to an alphabetic ordering of their citation-forms.

In order to assign a meaning to the word-forms of which a sentence is composed, we must be able to identify them, not merely as tokens of particular types, but as forms of particular expressions. And tokens of the same type are not necessarily forms of the same expression. For example, in the sentence

> 'They have found it impossible to found hospitals or charitable institutions of any kind without breaking the law',

the third and seventh word-tokens (*found*) are tokens of the same type, but not forms of the same expression. (I will employ the term 'word' to mean "word-expression", throughout the present work. Some linguists might disagree with this.)

Not all the expressions listed in a dictionary, however, are words. Some of them are *phrases*; and phrasal expressions, like word-expressions, must be distinguished in principle from the form or forms with which they are put into correspondence by the morphological rules of the language. For example, 'pass muster' is a phrasal expression, whose forms are *pass muster*, *passes muster*, *passed muster* etc. It is tokens of these forms that occur in sentences.

The expressions of a language fall into two sets. One set, of finite membership, is made up of *lexically simple* expressions: *lexemes*. These are the expressions that one would expect to find listed in a dictionary: they are the vocabulary-units of a language, out of which the members of the second set, *lexically composite* expressions, are constructed by means of the syntactic rules of the language. In terms of this distinction 'pass muster' is a lexeme, whereas 'pass the examination' is lexically composite.

Most word-expressions, in all languages, are lexically simple. However, in many languages there are productive rules for what is traditionally called *word-formation*, which enable their users to construct new word-expressions out of pre-existing lexically simpler expressions. For example, 'politeness' is constructed from the lexically simpler expression, 'polite', by means of a productive rule of English word-formation. Although many conventional dictionaries do in fact list 'politeness' as a vocabulary-unit, it is unnecessary to do so, since both its meaning and its grammatical properties (as well as its pronunciation) are predictable by rule.

Most phrasal expressions, in contrast with word-expressions, are lexically composite. Indeed, all well-studied natural languages furnish their users with the means of constructing an infinite number of lexically composite phrasal expressions. And, as we shall see later, it is an important principle of modern formal semantics that the meaning of all such lexically composite expressions should be systematically determinable on the basis of the meaning of the simpler expressions of which they are composed.

The distinction that has just been drawn between lexemes and lexically composite expressions is by no means as straightforward, in practice, as I have made it appear. But some such distinction is, and must be, drawn by anyone who concerns himself with the semantic analysis of natural languages. It is lexemes, rather than words and phrases as such, that will be at the centre of our attention in this and the next two chapters.

Homonymy and polysemy

What is traditionally described as *homonymy* was illustrated in Chapter 1 by means of the traditional examples of 'bank$_1$' and 'bank$_2$', the former meaning "financial institution" and the latter "sloping side of a river". The examples are appropriate enough. But the traditional definition of homonymy is, to say the least, imprecise.

Homonyms are traditionally defined as different words with the same form. We can immediately improve the definition, in the light of what was said in the preceding section, by substituting 'lexeme' for 'word'. But the definition is still defective in that it fails to take account of the fact that, in many languages, most lexemes have not one, but several, forms. Also, it says nothing about syntactic equivalence.

Let us begin, therefore, by drawing a distinction between *absolute homonymy*, on the one hand, and various kinds of *partial homonymy*, on the other. Absolute homonyms must satisfy the following three conditions: (i) their forms must be unrelated in meaning; (ii) all their forms must be identical (that is, the forms must be tokens of the same type); (iii) identical forms must be syntactically equivalent.

Absolute homonymy is common enough: cf. 'bank$_1$', 'bank$_2$'; 'sole$_1$' ("bottom of foot/shoe"), 'sole$_2$' ("kind of fish"); etc. But there are also many different kinds of partial homonymy. For example, 'find' and 'found' share the form *found*, but not *finds*, *finding* or *founds*, *founding* etc.; and *found* as a form of 'find' is not syntactically equivalent to *found* as a form of 'found'. In this case, as generally in English, the failure to satisfy (ii) correlates with the failure to satisfy (iii). However, it is important to realize that the last two conditions of absolute homonymy made explicit in the previous paragraph are logically independent. They are usually taken for granted without discussion in traditional accounts of the topic.

It is particularly important to note the condition of syntactic equivalence, and the fact that this is a matter of degree. Although *found* as a form of 'find' is not syntactically equivalent to *found* as a form of 'found', it is in both cases a verb-form. And there are certain contexts in which *found* may be construed, syntactically, in either way. For example,

'They found hospitals and charitable institutions' can be construed as a present-tense sentence containing a form of 'found' or, alternatively, as a past-tense sentence containing a form of 'find'. As a potential English utterance, it is ambiguous. And its ambiguity is, in part, lexical: it depends upon a difference in the meaning, in this case, of the two lexemes 'found' and 'find'.

The reasons why it is important for the semanticist to take note of the degree of syntactic equivalence is that, in general, this determines whether and to what degree homonymy results in ambiguity. If *have* is inserted before *found* ('They have found hospitals and charitable institutions') or, alternatively, if *he* or *she* is substituted for *they* ('He found hospitals and charitable institutions'), the ambiguity disappears. Ambiguity that results from absolute homonymy cannot be eliminated by manipulating the grammatical environment in this way. Moreover, it is quite possible for partial homonymy never to result in ambiguity: it may be that the shared forms are prohibited from occurring in the same syntactic environments. For example, the partial homonymy of the adjective 'last$_1$' (as in 'last week') and the verb 'last$_2$' (as in 'Bricks last a long time') rarely produces ambiguity. Their sole shared form, *last*, is almost always readily identifiable as a form of the one or the other by virtue of the syntactic environment in which it occurs.

We shall return to the question of ambiguity – and more particularly to the distinction between lexical and grammatical ambiguity – in a later chapter. It has been mentioned at this point because many general accounts of homonymy, both traditional and modern, fail to do justice to the fact that partial homonymy at least need not result in ambiguity.

They also fail to point out that partial homonymy does not necessarily involve identity of either the citation-forms or the underlying stem-forms of the lexemes in question. For example, the words 'rung' and 'ring' are partial homonyms, as in

'A rung of the ladder was broken';
'The bell was rung at midnight'.

Yet this kind of homonymy is often not recognized in standard treatments. Modern treatments of the question tend to be no better than more traditional accounts in this respect. The latter often concentrate on citation-forms, not surprisingly in view of the practical problems that confront the lexicographer in his day-to-day work. The former will frequently restrict the discussion, tacitly if not explicitly, to stem-forms. It so happens, of course, that in English the citation-forms coincide with the stem-form in all morphologically regular lexemes. But this is not so in languages in which stem-forms are bound rather than free.

Whereas homonymy (whether absolute or partial) is a relation that holds of two or more distinct lexemes, *polysemy* ("multiple meaning") is a property of single lexemes. This is how the distinction is commonly drawn. But everyone who draws this distinction also recognizes that, to quote one authority, 'the border-line . . . is sometimes fluid' (Ullmann, 1962: 159). It has been demonstrated that there is a good deal of agreement among native speakers as to what counts as the one and what counts as the other in particular instances. But there are also very many instances about which native speakers will hesitate or be in disagreement. What, then, is the difference in theory between homonymy and polysemy?

The two criteria that are usually invoked in this connexion have already been mentioned in Chapter 1: etymology (the historical source of the words) and relatedness of meaning. The main point to be made about the etymological criterion is that in general it supports the native speaker's untutored intuitions about particular lexemes. No one, for example, is likely to confuse 'bat$_1$' ("furry mammal with membraneous wings") with 'bat$_2$' ("implement for striking a ball in certain games"); and these two words do indeed differ in respect of their historical source, 'bat$_1$' being derived from a regional variant of Middle English 'bakke', and 'bat$_2$' from Old English 'batt' meaning "club, cudgel".

This is not to say that there are no exceptions. It is not uncommon for lexemes which the average speaker of the language thinks of as being semantically unrelated to have come from the same source. The homonyms 'sole$_1$' ("bottom of foot/shoe") and 'sole$_2$' ("kind of fish"), which I mentioned above, constitute a much-quoted example; and there are others, no less striking, to be found in the handbooks. Less common is the converse situation, where historically unrelated meanings are perceived by native speakers as having the same kind of connection as the distinguishable meanings of a single polysemous lexeme. But there are several examples of what, from a historical point of view, is quite clearly homonymy being reinterpreted by later generations of speakers as polysemy. It falls within the scope of what is commonly referred to by linguists as *popular etymology*. Today, for example, a number of speakers assume that 'shock$_1$' as in 'shock of corn' is the same as 'shock$_2$' as in 'shock of hair'. Yet historically, they have different origins.

There are exceptions, then, of both kinds. Nevertheless, the generalization that I have just made is undoubtedly correct: in most cases, etymology supports the average native speaker's intuitions about relatedness of meaning. As we shall see presently, there are good reasons why this should be so. One of the principal factors operative in semantic change is metaphorical extension, as when 'foot', "terminal part of leg", was extended to "lowest part of mountain". And it is metaphorical extension as a synchronic process that is at issue when one refers to the related meanings of polysemous lexemes. There are, of course, other kinds of relatedness of meaning, which are irrelevant in this connection. But metaphorical creativity (in the broadest sense of 'metaphorical') is part of everyone's linguistic competence. In the last resort, it is impossible to draw a sharp distinction between the spontaneous extension or transfer of meaning by individual speakers on particular occasions and their use of the pre-existing, or institutionalized, extended and transferred meanings of a lexeme that are to be found in a dictionary. This fact has important implications for linquistic theory that go way beyond the traditional, and perhaps insoluble, problem of distinguishing polysemy from homonymy.

Full and empty word-forms

The word-forms of English, like the word-forms of most languages, can be put into two classes. One class consists of full forms like *man*, *came*, *green*, *badly*; the other of empty forms like *the*, *of*, *and*, *to*, *if*. The distinction between the two classes is not always clear-cut. But it is intuitively recognizable in the examples that I have just given. And it has been drawn on non-intuitive grounds, by applying a variety of criteria, by linguists of different theoretical persuasions. Essentially the same distinction was drawn, centuries ago, in the Chinese grammatical tradition; at the end of the nineteenth century, by the English grammarian, Henry Sweet (better known these days, no doubt, as the model for Professor Higgins in *Pygmalion* and *My Fair Lady*); and at the height of post-Bloomfieldian structuralism, in the 1950s, by the American linguist, C.C. Fries.

The terms that I have chosen, taken from the Chinese tradition, emphasize the intuitively evident semantic difference between typical members of one class and typical members of the other. Empty word-forms may not be entirely devoid of meaning (though some of them are in certain contexts). But they generally have less meaning than full word-forms do: they are more easily predictable in the contexts in which they occur. Hence their omission in headlines, telegrams etc., and perhaps also in the utterances of very young children as they pass through early stages of language-acquisition. Other terms found in the literature for empty word-forms are 'form words', 'function words' and 'structural words'.

Not only do empty word-forms tend to be less meaningful than full word-forms. Their meaning seems to be different from, and more heterogeneous than, that of full word-forms. This difference between the two classes comes out immediately in relation to some of the theories of meaning mentioned in Chapter 1. It is perhaps reasonable enough to say that *dog* (i.e., one of the forms of 'dog') refers to a class of objects or, alternatively, to its defining property. Or again, that the meaning of *dog* is the associated concept or behavioural response. It hardly makes sense to talk of the meaning of *the*, *of*, *and*, *to* and *if* in such terms.

The point that has just been made is often presented as if it were a damaging point of criticism against any theory of word-meaning which defines it to be something other than its contribution to sentence-meaning. It is asserted, correctly, that the meaning of empty word-forms, no less than that of full word-forms, can be brought within the scope of the following general principle: the meaning of a form is the contribution it makes to the meaning of the sentences in which it occurs. It is then argued, fallaciously, that because the meaning of such forms as *the*, *of*, *and*, *to* and *if* cannot be defined otherwise than in terms of sentence-meaning, sentence-meaning is always logically prior to word-meaning. The conclusion may or may not be correct: we shall return to this question of logical priority later. But the argument is fallacious, because it rests upon the spurious methodological principle that all words must have the same kind of meaning. Also, it trades upon the fact that the term 'word' denotes both forms and expressions; and empty word-forms are neither expressions nor forms of expressions.

Actually, the distinction between full word-forms and empty word-forms is no more than the product of several more technical distinctions, which I will not go into here. What is really at issue is the distinction between the grammar of a language and its *lexicon*. The latter may be thought of as the theoretical counterpart of a dictionary, and it is frequently so described. Looked at from a psychological point of view, the lexicon is the set of all the lexemes in a language, stored in the brains of competent speakers, with all the linguistic information for each lexeme that is required for the production and interpretation of the sentences of the language. Very little is known so far, in psychological terms, about the so-called mental lexicon, just as relatively little is known in detail about the mental grammar that we all carry around with us in our heads. In particular, it is not known whether there is a clear-cut psychological distinction to be drawn between grammar and lexicon. At any rate, linguists have so far found it impossible to draw any such distinction sharply in the description of particular languages.

All that needs to be said here is that some, though not all, of the so-called empty word-forms will have a purely grammatical meaning (if they have any meaning at all), whereas all the full word-forms will have both a lexical and a grammatical meaning. For example, *child* and *children*, being forms of the same lexeme, have the same lexical meaning. Insofar as the lexeme has certain semantically relevant grammatical properties (it is a noun of particular kind), the two word-forms also share some of their grammatical meaning. But they differ, of course, from this point of view, in that the one is a singular and the other a plural noun-form. It is lexical meaning that we are discussing in Part 2. Grammatical meaning, not all of which can be assigned to word-forms, is largely a matter of sentence-meaning, and will therefore be dealt with in Part 3.

Synonymy

Expressions with the same meaning are *synonymous*. Two points should be noted about this definition. First, it does not restrict the relation of synonymy to lexemes: it allows for the possibility that lexically simple expressions may have the same meaning as lexically complex expressions. Second, it makes identity, not merely similarity, of meaning the criterion of synonymy.

In this latter respect, it differs from the definition of synonymy that will be found in standard dictionaries and the one with which lexicographers themselves customarily operate. Many of the expressions listed as synonymous in ordinary or specialized dictionaries (including *Roget's Thesaurus* and other dictionaries of synonyms and antonyms) are what may be called *near-synonyms*: expressions that are more or less similar, but not identical, in meaning. Near-synonymy, as we shall see, is not to be confused with various kinds of partial synonymy, which meet our criterion of identity of meaning.

It is by now almost axiomatic in linguistics that *absolute synonymy*, as I shall define it, is extremely rare – at least as a relation between lexemes – in natural languages. Let us therefore distinguish *partial synonymy* from absolute synonymy in terms of the failure of synonymous expressions to satisfy one or more of the following conditions:

(i)   synonyms are *fully* synonymous if, and only if, *all their meanings* are identical;

(ii) synonyms are *totally* synonymous if, and only if, they are synonymous *in all contexts*;

(iii) synonyms are *completely synonymous* if, and only if,
they are identical *on all* (*relevant*) *dimensions of
meaning*.

Although one or more of these conditions are commonly
mentioned in discussions of synonymy it is seldom pointed
out that they are logically independent of one another.

There is the further problem that the very terms
'absolute synonymy', 'full synonymy', 'total synonymy'
and 'complete synonymy' (not to mention 'exact synonymy') are themselves frequently employed as
synonyms, whether absolute or partial, in standard works
– usually without definition. In terms of the definitions
given here, absolute synonyms are expressions that are
fully, totally and completely synonymous; partial
synonyms are synonymous, but not absolutely so. I am
not concerned with the proliferation of hair-splitting
terminological distinctions for their own sake. But I do
wish to insist upon the importance of: (a) not confusing
near-synonymy with partial synonymy; and (b) not making the assumption that failure to satisfy one of the
conditions of absolute synonymy necessarily involves the
failure to satisfy either or both of the other conditions.
Let us take each of the conditions of absolute synonymy
in turn.

Standard dictionaries of English treat the adjectives
'big' and 'large' as polysemous (though they vary in the
number of meanings that they assign to each). In one
meaning, exemplified by
'They live in a big/large house',
the two words are, I believe, synonymous. Whether they
are completely synonymous is a question to which we
shall return. It is easy to show, however, that 'big' and
'large' are not fully synonymous. The following sentence,
'I will tell my big sister',
is lexically ambiguous, by virtue of the polysemy of 'big',
in a way that
'I will tell my large sister'

is not. All three sentences are well-formed and interpretable. They show that 'big' has at least one meaning that it does not share with 'large'. So, in terms of criterion (i) (having the same range of meanings), and on the assumption that 'big' and 'large' are indeed synonymous in one of their meanings in the sentences above, they are not fully synonymous. There are many such examples.

Let us now turn to total synonymy. What is at issue here is the *collocational* range of an expression: the set of contexts in which it can occur. It might be thought that the collocational range of an expression is determined by its meaning, so that synonyms must of necessity have the same collocational range. But this does not seem to be so. For example, a recent work on modern linguistics draws attention to the three words 'flaw', 'defect' and 'blemish', which appear to have the same meaning and yet are not interchangeable. The authors point out that, whereas it is normal to use either 'blemish' or 'flaw', of someone's complexion and either 'flaw' or 'defect' of someone's argument, it would be odd to use 'blemish' of someone's reasoning (Smith and Wilson, 1979: 52). This is similar to the case of 'big' and 'large', which are neither fully nor totally synonymous. There are many contexts in which 'large' and 'big' are not interchangeable without violating the collocational restrictions of the one or the other. For example, 'large' cannot be substituted for 'big' in

'You are making a big mistake'.

And yet 'big' seems to have the same meaning here as it does in phrases such as 'a big house', for which we could, as we have seen, substitute 'a large house'.

It is tempting to argue, in cases like this, that there must be some subtle difference of lexical meaning which accounts for the collocational differences, such that it is not synonymy, but near-synonymy, that is involved. Very often, undoubtedly, collocational differences can be satisfactorily explained in terms of independently ascertainable differences of meaning. But this is not always so.

Let us now turn briefly to the difference between

complete and incomplete synonymy, in terms of (iii) (similarity of all relevant dimensions of meaning). The most widely recognized dimension of meaning that is relevant to this distinction is that of *descriptive* (or propositional) meaning (see Chapter 1). In fact, many theories of semantics would restrict the notion of synonymy to what I will call descriptive synonymy: identity of descriptive meaning. What precisely is meant by identity of descriptive meaning is a question that will be taken up, in Part 3. For the present, it will be sufficient to say that two expressions have the same descriptive meaning (i.e., are descriptively synonymous) if, and only if, statements containing the one necessarily imply otherwise identical statements containing the other, and vice versa. By this criterion 'big' and 'large' are descriptively synonymous (in one of their meanings and over a certain range of contexts). For instance, I cannot without contradiction simultaneously assert that someone lives in a big house and deny that he lives in a large house.

The classic example of descriptive synonymy is the relation that holds in English between 'bachelor' and 'unmarried man'. There are those who would deny that these two expressions are, in fact, descriptively synonymous, on the grounds that a divorced man, though unmarried, is not a bachelor. The point is debatable, and I will return to it. But the principle that the example is intended to illustrate is clear enough. We test for descriptive synonymy by finding out whether anyone truly described as a bachelor is truly describable as an unmarried man, and vice versa. It may well be that for some speakers the expressions are synonymous and for others they are not, and that for a third group the situation is unclear. Those who hold that 'unmarried' does not mean simply "not married" and cannot be correctly applied to divorcees – together with those, if any, who would readily apply both 'bachelor' and 'unmarried' to divorcees – will treat 'bachelor' and 'unmarried man' as descriptively synonymous.

When it comes to *expressive* meaning – and this is the only kind of non-descriptive meaning that we will take into account at this point – there is no readily available and reasonably objective criterion which enables us to decide between identity and difference. But it is nonetheless possible, in particular instances, to determine that two or more descriptively synonymous expressions differ in respect of the degree or nature of their expressive meaning. For example, it is intuitively obvious that a whole set of words including 'huge', 'enormous', 'gigantic' and 'colossal' are more expressive of their users' feelings towards what they are describing than 'very big' or 'very large', with which they are perhaps descriptively synonymous. It is more difficult to compare 'huge', 'enormous', 'gigantic' and 'colossal' among themselves in terms of their degree of expressivity. But speakers may have clear intuitions about two or more of them; and the question is, in principle, decidable by means of relatively objective psychological tests.

As to expressions which differ in the nature of their expressive meaning, the most obvious difference is between those which imply approval or disapproval and those which are neutral with respect to expressivity, or imply the opposite attitude. The handbooks are full of examples, such as 'statesman' *vs* 'politician'; 'thrifty' *vs* 'mean'/ 'stingy' *vs* 'economical'; 'stink'/'stench' *vs* 'fragrance' *vs* 'smell'; 'crafty'/'cunning' *vs* 'skilful' *vs* 'clever'; and so on. In many cases, the fact that an expression implies approval or disapproval is much more readily ascertainable than is its descriptive meaning (if it has any). This is true, for example, of words like 'bitch' or 'swine' used in what was once, but is perhaps no longer for most speakers of English, their metaphorical sense. Under what conditions can one truly describe a person as a bitch or swine? In cases like this it is surely the expressive, rather than the descriptive, component of meaning that is dominant.

Most of the lexemes in everyday use have both a

descriptive and an expressive meaning. Indeed, as certain philosophers of language have pointed out in respect of the vocabulary of moral and aesthetic statements, it may be even theoretically impossible at times to separate the descriptive from the expressive. However that may be, knowing the expressive meaning of a lexeme is just as much a part of one's competence in a language as knowing its descriptive meaning. This point should be borne in mind, even though we shall be concerned almost exclusively with descriptive meaning in our treatment of lexical structure in Chapter 3.

My main purpose, in the brief account of synonymy that has been given here, has been to emphasize the theoretical importance of distinguishing the several kinds of partial synonymy from one another and from near-synonymy. In doing so, I have been obliged to gloss over a number of difficulties and complications that a more comprehensive discussion of synonymy would require us to deal with. Some of these will be mentioned in Chapter 4, as far as descriptive synonymy is concerned, in connection with the notion of entailment.

Summary

In this chapter, I have dealt with various facets and hidden complications of the word 'word', insofar as these are relevant to the investigation of meaning. I have also discussed, in outline, some of the problems raised by the phenomena of homonymy, polysemy and synonymy. With these matters cleared away, we can now move on to discuss the question of definitions.

3 Dealing with Definitions

The difficulty of defining words

'To define true madness,
What is't but to be nothing else but mad?'
William Shakespeare, *Hamlet*

'I hate definitions' is a saying attributed to Benjamin Disraeli. If his aim was to point out the extreme difficulty of defining words, one must sympathize with him. The problem is a profound one, as we shall see in this chapter, which discusses some of the proposals that have been put forward for dealing with the definitions of words.

Suppose a foreigner who did not know English asked you what the word 'table' means. Would you utter the word-form *table* and point to several different kinds of tables, in the hope that he would not assume you were indicating that 'table' is a general word meaning "furniture"? Would you try to teach him the words 'chair' and 'desk' as well, so that he would be sure to distinguish tables from desks and chairs? Or would you show him some people sitting round a table having a meal, on the assumption that the definition of 'table' should include some guidance as to what a table is used for? All these proposals have been put forward in the literature. As we shall see, they all present problems; and no single one of them, to the exclusion of the others, is acceptable. Indeed, the whole question of definition is far more complex – and a good deal more interesting – than most people realize. Madness it may be to define not only 'madness', but any word at all. We can still learn a lot about the nature of word-meaning by looking at the theory and practice of definition.

Denotation and sense

Let us suppose that we are asked to define the word 'dog', taking no account of anything other than its descriptive meaning. There are two ways of going about this. The first is to identify, for the benefit of our enquirer, all those entities in the world of which the proposition "That is a dog" is true. This is to define the *denotation* of 'dog'. How we might, in practice, identify everything and anything that is denoted by 'dog' is a question that we will take up presently. The important point for the moment is that some words, if not all, may be put into correspondence with classes of entities in the external world.

Denotation, as we shall see later, is intrinsically connected with *reference*. Indeed, many authorities would draw no distinction between them, subsuming both under a broader notion of reference. However it is intuitively obvious that 'dog' does not stand for the class of dogs or, alternatively, for some defining property of this class in quite the same way that 'Fido' can be used to stand for, or *refer* to, some particular dog. The crudest version of the referential theory of meaning, which Ryle aptly dubbed the 'Fido'-Fido theory, will not work for anything other than proper names. There are more sophisticated versions of the theory, which would justify the adoption of a broader notion of reference than I shall be employing in this book. But, initially at least, it is important to insist upon the difference in the way that lexemes and referring expressions hook on to the world. The denotation of a lexeme belongs to the lexeme independently of its use on particular occasions of utterance; the reference of a referring expression will usually vary from one context of use to another. For example, the word 'dog' denotes a particular class of animals, whereas the phrases 'the dog' or 'my dog' or 'the dog that bit the postman' will refer to different members of the class on different occasions of utterance. Reference, as distinct from denotation, will be dealt with in a later chapter.

The lexeme 'dog', then, denotes a class of entities in the external world. But it is also related, in various ways, to other words and expressions of English, including 'animal'; 'hound', 'terrier', 'spaniel', etc.; 'bitch'; 'fox', 'wolf', etc.; 'cat', 'pig', 'sheep', 'horse', etc. Each relation of this kind that holds between 'dog' and other expressions, may be identified as one of its sense-relations. Descriptive synonymy, which we discussed in the last chapter, is one kind of *sense-relation*. We shall look briefly at some of the other sense-relations exemplified above for 'dog' in the following chapter. Meanwhile, the examples themselves will suffice for the purpose of explaining both the distinction between denotation and sense and, no less important, their interdependence.

The *sense* of an expression is, quite simply, the set of sense-relations that hold between it and other expressions. Several points may now be made in respect of this definition. First, sense is a matter of relations that hold among linguistic expressions: that is to say, among entities all of which belong to one language or another. This distinguishes it clearly from denotation, which relates expressions to classes of entities in the world.

What has just been said is not invalidated by the existence, in all natural languages, of various kinds of metalinguistic expressions; and this point must be emphasized. The distinction between sense and denotation applies to metalinguistic expressions such as 'lexeme', 'word', or 'linguistic expression' in exactly the same way as it applies to other expressions. Admittedly, it is much harder to keep one's thinking straight in the case of metalinguistic expressions than it is in respect of expressions that denote dogs and cats and other such denizens of the external world. Nevertheless, it should be clear upon reflection, if not immediately, that linguistic expressions such as 'linguistic expression' and 'lexeme' are related to one another in terms of sense in the way that 'animal' and 'dog' are, whereas 'linguistic expression' and 'lexeme' are related in terms of denotation in the same way as 'animal' and some particular dog or other animal. For example, just as 'animal' denotes the dogs Fido, Rover, etc., as well as other subclasses of the class of animals, so 'linguistic expression' denotes the linguistic expressions 'linguistic expression', 'lexeme', 'word', etc., as well as, say, 'dog', 'animal', etc. Denotation, as we have seen, is a relation which holds primarily, or basically, between expressions and physical entities in the external world. But natural languages also contain expressions which denote non-physical entities. Although metalinguistic expressions are not the only such expressions, they are of particular interest to the semanticist.

The second point that needs to be made explicit about sense and denotation is that both notions apply equally to lexically simple and lexically composite expressions. For example, 'domesticated canine mammal' and 'common four-legged flesh-eating animal', taken from the entries for 'dog' in two recently published dictionaries, are lexically composite expressions, whose sense and denotation are determined by the sense and denotation of their constituent lexemes. They are interestingly different in that the one makes use of more specialized lexemes ('canine' and 'mammal') than the other; and we shall return to this aspect of the question presently. In both cases, however, the general principle holds, that the sense and denotation of the whole is a *compositional function* of the sense and denotation of the parts: this principle will be explained in Chapter 4.

A third point, which is perhaps obvious but, like the preceding one, will be important later and needs to be clearly stated, is that sense and denotation are, in general, interdependent and inversely related in terms of size. They are interdependent in that (in the case of expressions that have both sense and denotation) one would not normally know the one without having at least some knowledge of the other. This raises the possibility that either sense or denotation should be taken to be logically or psychologically more basic than the other. I will take up this possibility in the following section.

As for the inverse relation that holds between sense and denotation, this can be expressed informally as follows: the larger the denotation, the smaller the sense, and conversely. For example, the denotation of 'animal' is larger than that of 'dog' (all dogs are animals, but not all animals are dogs), but the sense of 'animal' is less specific than that of 'dog'. This inverse relation is well recognized in traditional logic in terms of the difference between extension and intension: roughly speaking, the *extension* of a term, or expression, is the class of entities that it defines, and the *intension* is the defining property of the class. Modern formal semantics, as we shall see, develops this distinction in a particular way.

Finally, as far as this section is concerned, it must be emphasized that nothing said here about sense and denotation is to be taken as implying that either the one or the other is fully determinate in the case of all, or even most, lexemes in the vocabularies of natural languages. On the contrary, the sense of most lexemes, and therefore of most lexically composite expressions, would seem to be somewhat fuzzy at the edges. Similarly, it is very often unclear whether a particular entity falls within the denotation of an expression or not. What then does it mean to say that someone knows the descriptive meaning of particular expressions in his native language? Indeed, how do we manage to communicate with one another more or less successfully, by means of language, if the descriptive meaning of most lexemes – their sense and denotation – is inherently fuzzy or indeterminate? Let us keep this question in mind.

Basic and non-basic expressions

Some forty years ago, Bertrand Russell drew a distinction, which has subsequently been much discussed by semanticists, between what he called object-words and dictionary words. The distinction itself was by no means original. But Russell expressed himself with characteristic lucidity, and the way in which he developed the underlying, initially appealing, principle makes his formulation of the distinction particularly interesting. Object-words, he tells us, 'are defined, logically as words having meaning in isolation, and psychologically, as words which have been learnt without its being necessary to have previously learnt any other words.' Dictionary words, in contrast, "are theoretically superfluous", since they are definable, and may be learned, in terms of the logically and psychologically more basic object-words (Russell, 1941: 62–3).

Leaving the non-basic dictionary words on one side for the moment, we may now ask how one comes to know the descriptive meaning of the allegedly basic object-words. Russell is quite clear, not to say dogmatic, on this point. Object-words are learned by *ostension:* that is, by showing the learner a sufficient number of entities that fall within the denotation, or extension, of each object-word. At its most explicit, *ostensive definition* would involve pointing at one or more entities denoted by the word in question and saying, "That is (an) X": for example, pointing at one or more dogs and saying, "That is a dog". Ostensive definition plays a prominent role, in theory if not in practice, in the empiricist tradition, to which Russell belonged. So too does denotation. And Russell's definition of object-words makes it clear that their meaning, in contrast with that of dictionary words, is wholly a matter of denotation.

But the notion of ostensive definition has come in for a lot of criticism. In fact, it is readily shown to be indefensible in the form in which Russell and other empiricist philosophers have assumed it to operate. First of all, the person for whom an expression is being defined ostensively must understand the meaning of the demonstrative pronoun 'that' (or its equivalent in other languages) in the proposition "That is (an) X", or alternatively of the gesture that serves the same purpose. He must also realize what more general purpose is being served by the utterance or gesture in question; it is easy to overlook the importance of this component of the process of ostensive definition. Finally, he must not only appreciate that the entity to which his attention is being drawn, ostensively, is to be considered as an example of some class, but also either know in advance or infer the intension (defining property) of the class that is being exemplified. Every entity exemplifies a potentially infinite set of classes. For example, our friend Fido is a member of the class of dogs, but he is also a member of indefinitely many of its subclasses (spaniels, dogs with drooping ears, dogs with short legs, dogs with a doleful expression, dogs with reddish-brown hair, etc.); of indefinitely many of its superclasses (mammals, four-legged creatures, animals, physical entities, etc.); and, most important of all, of indefinitely many classes of entities to which few, if any, other dogs, but lots of non-dogs may belong (e.g., the class of mobile entities that make a recognizable sound and cause little Johnny to coo with pleasure: Mummy, Daddy, the cat, the vacuum cleaner, etc.). How can one tell just which of this potentially infinite set of classes is the one that is being defined?

The problem is not insoluble, if we assume that the person learning the extension of an expression (the class of entities it denotes) has prior knowledge of what its intension is likely to be. For the out-and-out empiricist, however, the problem does seem to be insoluble.

Let us now drop what I will refer to as Russell's condition of atomicity: the condition imposed upon object-words that their meaning should be logically and psychologically independent of the meaning of other words. It is much easier to get someone to see what one is pointing to and to give him some idea of the class that is intended to be exemplified by the entity indicated, if one allows oneself to use other expressions, basic or non-basic, that are related in sense to the word one is defining.

For example, if I say, not "That is a dog", but "That animal is a dog", my interlocutor (on the assumption that he has a sufficiently good knowledge of the intension of 'animal') is less likely to think I am pointing at the vacuum cleaner or the hearth rug. If I say "That is a dog – not a cat", I thereby draw his attention to those features, both phenomenal and functional, which distinguish dogs from cats. In short, ostensive definition is much more likely to be successful if the condition of atomicity is dropped.

Anyway, regardless of whether it is in principle possible to learn the denotation of one expression without knowing (or simultaneously learning) the denotation of other expressions to which it is related in sense, it seems clear that we do not operate in this way in practice. We do not, as children, first learn the full extension of, let us say, 'red' without knowing anything of the extension of 'brown' or 'pink'. We do not learn the full extension of 'dog' without knowing anything of the extension of some of the more commonly occurring expressions that are related to it in sense. Russell claimed, it will be recalled, that object words 'are defined ... psychologically, as words which have been learnt without its being necessary to have previously learnt any other words.' If 'psychologically' in Russell's definition is understood to make reference to the acquisition of language by children under normal conditions, then the sense and denotation of what Russell and others might think of as basic words are certainly not psychologically independent of one another. (Incidentally, Russell's own examples, from English, include 'man', 'dog', 'yellow', 'hard', 'sweet'; 'walk', 'run', 'eat', 'drink'; 'up', 'down', 'in', 'out', 'before', 'after'.) Child language-acquisition has been intensively investigated in recent years, and it is clear that children do not learn the meaning of words in the way that Russell suggests. A famous case in the literature concerns a child who said *kwa* (the child's version of *quack*) not only to refer to a duck, but also to milk, a coin, and a teddy bear's eye. A child gradually learns the denotation of one word only by simultaneously learning the denotation of other words.

Where does this leave us, then, as far as the distinction between basic and non-basic expressions is concerned? It has a long history and, as I said earlier, it is intuitively appealing. Obviously, if the argument of the last few paragraphs is accepted, we cannot go along with Russell and say that basic expressions are those whose sense is fully determined by their denotation and that non-basic expressions are those whose sense (which subsequently determines their denotation) is fully determined by the sense of the basic expressions used to define them.

But this does not mean that the distinction itself falls to the ground. After all, it is the very foundation stone of the very practical system known as Basic English, invented by C.K. Ogden in the 1930s and intended as an international second language. Basic English has a vocabulary of 850 lexemes; and these are held to be sufficient for the definition of the other lexemes of Standard English, not to mention all the lexemes of other languages. And Basic English is one of several such systems which derive ultimately from the philosophical speculations of Leibniz, Bishop Wilkins and other seventeenth-century scholars, whose works informed the tradition of logical empiricism to which Russell belonged and exerted a powerful influence upon Roget, when he compiled his famous *Thesaurus of English Words and Phrases* in 1852. Also, without making any philosophical claims for the allegedly basic vocabulary with which they operate, many foreign-language manuals deliberately restrict themselves to what they consider to be basic, in the sense of being necessary and sufficient for everyday purposes. In some countries, and for some languages, basic word-lists of this kind have been officially promulgated, and text-books and examinations are geared to them.

As for dictionary words, it is interesting to return now to the lexically composite expressions taken from the entries for 'dog' in two recent dictionaries of English and cited in the previous section: 'domesticated canine mammal' and 'common four-legged flesh-eating animal'. The former comes from the *Collins Dictionary of the English Language* (1979); the latter from the *Longman Dictionary of Contemporary English* (1978). The most striking difference between them is that the Longman definition is written in words selected from 'a controlled vocabulary of approximately 2000 words which were selected by a thorough study of a number of frequency and pedagogic lists' and conforms to the principle that 'definitions are always written using simpler terms than the words they describe' (pp. viii–ix), whereas the Collins definition is written with respect to the different, but not incompatible, principle that it should be 'in lucid English prose' and should be written with words each of which 'is itself an entry in the dictionary' (p. xv). Another difference, which will be relevant in the following section, is that the Collins expression is closer to being synonymous with 'dog' (in one of its meanings) than the Longman expression.

Here I want to emphasize the fact that there are at least two different senses of 'basic' (or 'simple') in which one lexeme may be more basic (or simpler) than another. The more obvious sense of 'basic' is that which depends upon frequency of occurrence in everyday, non-technical, usage. By this criterion the Longman entry clearly contains more basic (and simpler) words than the Collins entry does – though it also requires the user to interpret the lexically composite expressions 'four-legged' and 'flesh-eating'. The deliberately restricted vocabulary of the foreign-language manuals referred to above can be called basic in the same sense.

In principle, however, there is another sense of 'basic'. In this second sense, it is by no means clear that familiar, everyday words are necessarily more basic than less familiar words like 'mammal' or 'domesticated'. Some words might be more basic than others in that they can be used to define a greater proportion of the total vocabulary or can be used to construct a more elegant and systematic set of inter-connected definitions. They might be more directly associated with what Leibniz and other seventeenth-century philosophers have thought of as *atomic concepts*: the building blocks, as it were, of the conceptual system which guides and constrains all thinking and rational discourse. This is the sense of 'basic', or 'primary', that is dominant in the philosophical tradition, though Russell and others frequently talk as if the two senses will determine much the same set of object-words. It is also this second sense of 'basic' that has been dominant, as we shall see in Chapter 4, in a good deal of recent theorizing in linguistics. There is no reason to believe that the two senses of 'basic' should be applicable to exactly the same lexemes. But it is reasonable to assume that many of the lexemes in the vocabularies of all natural languages should be basic in both senses. We shall keep this point in mind in our discussion of natural kinds and semantic proto-types.

In this section, I have deliberately introduced and emphasized some philosophical ideas which are rarely mentioned in introductions to semantics written by linguists. I have done this because, in my view, it is impossible to evaluate even the most down-to-earth work in descriptive semantics unless one has some notion of the general philosophical framework within which it is written. This holds true regardless of whether the author himself is aware of the philosophical origins or implications of his working principles.

It remains to add that the empiricist tradition has been immensely important in the development of modern formal semantics and continues to influence the thinking of many who are most vociferous in their rejection of empiricism. Empiricist philosophers have always tended to give priority to the *phenomenal* attributes of entities in their discussion of denotation: i.e., to those attributes that can be known or perceived through the senses. We must be careful not to accept this point of view, uncritically, simply because it has been passed on to us, often no less uncritically, by tradition. The *functional* attributes – those attributes that make them useful to us for particular purposes – are no less important in the determination of what is, or might be, basic in the vocabulary of human languages. For example, edibility is likely to be as important as colour or shape, and just as likely to serve as one of the properties which we recognize as criterial in establishing the denotation of whole sets of lexemes.

Natural kinds and semantic proto-types

The naive monolingual speaker of English, or of any other language, is often surprised when he is told that there are lexemes in his language that cannot be matched with descriptively equivalent lexemes in other languages. And yet this is true. Nor should it be thought that it is only words denoting culturally or geographically restricted classes of entities (e.g., 'shrine', 'boomerang', 'monsoon', 'willow', etc.) that lack their descriptive equivalents. There is plenty of snow in Greenland; there is no dearth of sand in the Australian desert; and camels are ubiquitous in most of the Arabic-speaking countries. Nevertheless, there is no single, general, word for snow in Eskimo, no word for sand in many of the aboriginal languages of Australia, no word for camels as such in Arabic. Examples like this find their place in almost every textbook of linguistics written in the last fifty years. Indeed, as one trots out yet again the Eskimo and Arabic examples, one finds it difficult to refrain from prefacing them with 'as every schoolboy (and schoolgirl) knows'!

But we do not have to take our examples from what many would regard as exotic languages. Despite the impression that might be given by standard bilingual dictionaries, such common English words as 'brown', 'monkey', 'chair', 'jug', 'carpet' – to take but a few – cannot be translated exactly into French, out of context and without making more or less arbitrary choices.

According to context, 'brown' will be translated into French (or should be) sometimes with 'brun' and sometimes with 'marron', not to mention 'beige' and similar more specific words. There are even occasions, notably with reference to men's shoes, when 'brown' (if we know that it refers to a particularly light shade) might well be translated with 'jaune', which we usually think of as meaning "yellow". And there are numerous other examples (some of which I have discussed elsewhere).

These lexical differences between languages are frequently summarized by linguists with the following generalization: every language divides up the world, or reality, in its own way. A more controversial formulation of the same point, associated in recent years with the names of the American linguists Edward Sapir and Benjamin Lee Whorf, is that what we think of as the world, or reality, is very largely the product of the categories imposed upon the mush of experience and the amorphous flow of thought by the languages we happen to speak. Essentially the same view was taken, at the turn of the century, by the Swiss linguist, Ferdinand de Saussure, and is a common, though not an essential, component in various kinds of *structuralism*, both European and American.

Structuralism may be contrasted, in this respect, with *atomism* (cf. the condition of atomicity, and the notion of atomic concepts mentioned in the previous section): it emphasizes the interdependence of entities, rather than their individual and separate existence. Indeed, structuralism as a philosophical doctrine maintains in its extreme form that entities have no essence or existence independently of the structure that is imposed by thought or language upon some otherwise undifferentiated world-stuff. It is a heady doctrine, and many semanticists have been intoxicated by it. Diluted with a sufficient measure of naive realism, it is palatable to all but the most eccentric of philosophical tastes, and still distinctive enough to be worth recommending.

Naive realism may differ from philosophical realism.

But supporters of each are at one in their belief that the external world is made up of entities whose existence is independent of the mind and of language. Furthermore, they would agree that some or all of these entities (persons, animals, things) can be grouped into what are traditionally called *natural kinds*: i.e., classes whose members share the same essence. The most obvious candidates for the status of natural kinds are, of course, living species, which reproduce themselves, each according to its kind, as the traditional expression goes. We find human beings begetting and giving birth to human beings; tigers producing new tigers; oak trees reproducing their kind essentially unchanged; and so on. According to the realist, the external world also contains aggregates of different kinds of stuff – water, gold, salt, etc. – such that any two aggregates of stuff are wholly or partly of the same kind or not. Traditional grammar, which was strongly realist in philosophical inspiration throughout most of its history, would say that, whereas proper names denote individual entities, common (i.e., non-proper) nouns denote natural kinds. English, like some but not all languages, draws a grammatical distinction between entity-denoting words, *countable nouns* ('man', 'tiger', 'oak tree') and stuff-denoting words, *mass nouns* ('water', 'gold', 'salt').

Until recently, most philosophers of language who have subscribed to the traditional doctrine of natural kinds have interpreted it in terms of the distinction between intension and extension. They have said that to know the meaning of any expression that denotes a natural kind (i.e., to know its sense) is to know its intension: its defining property, or, in philosophical terms, the necessary and sufficient conditions that must be satisfied by any entity or stuff that falls within the extension of the expression in question. In the last few years, an interestingly new version of the doctrine of natural kinds has been proposed, notably by Hilary Putnam and Saul Kripke, which severs the connection between intension and essence. We cannot go further into the philosophical issues. But for those readers with the requisite background in philosophy, it may be noted that the theory of natural-kind expressions, as developed by Putnam and Kripke, transcends the age-old dispute between nominalists and realists: it is a nominalist's theory, in that it takes the association between a natural-kind expression and its extension to be, in all crucial respects, identical with the association between a proper name and its bearer; it is a realist's theory, in that it does not deny that members of the same natural kind share the same essence. The arguments deployed by Putnam, Kripke and their followers are subtle and persuasive; and they are backed up with all the technicalities of modern mathematical logic. (References are given in the Bibliography at the end of this book.)

Ideally, we would require any good theory of semantics to fit in with everyday, non-technical accounts of descriptive meaning (and the Putnam and Kripke approach mentioned above does just this). That is, we do not want a theory of semantics which goes against commonsense accounts of the kind that the man in the Clapham omnibus might give, as long as one does not bemuse him, or, as Wittgenstein would have said, start his mind idling, by putting to him abstract general questions like "What is meaning?". If knowing the descriptive meaning of 'dog' involves knowing the defining characteristics of the natural kind that it denotes, few, if any, speakers of English can be said to know the meaning of 'dog'. There are experts, recognized as such in the culture to which we belong, who can arbitrate for us in dubious cases (for example, if I am prosecuted on the grounds that I have wilfully allowed my dog to foul the pavement and I deny that it is a dog). But even the experts may disagree among themselves. The descriptive meaning of natural-kind expressions, like the decriptive meaning of most lexemes, is inherently fuzzy or indeterminate. We communicate with one another for the most part successfully, as far as the application of words like 'dog' are concerned, only because we do not usually find ourselves operating in the fuzzy or indeterminate areas of a word's meaning.

Generally speaking, we operate with what have come to be called *proto-types*, or stereotypes; and usually what we want to refer to conforms to the proto-type. For example, the proto-type for 'dog' might be rather like the Longman definition, which was contrasted with the Collins definition in the previous section: "a common four-legged flesh-eating animal, especially any of the many varieties used by man as a companion or for hunting, working, guarding, etc,". I have now quoted the definition in full; and it will be observed that the additional part of the definition, running from "especially" to "etc.", indicates that there are several varieties of dogs and that some of these fall within the *focal extension* of 'dog' (that is, they are more typical sub-classes of the class than other, non-focal, varieties are). As for the varieties, we could all name a few, and dog-fanciers a lot more: spaniels, terriers, poodles etc. When we say that someone knows the meaning of 'dog', we imply that he has just this kind of knowledge. As I pointed out earlier, the Longman definition unlike the Collins definition ('domesticated canine mammal') does not claim to be synonymous with what it defines. But this is not necessarily a flaw. Sometimes the descriptive meaning of a lexeme can be explained by means of a more or less synonymous paraphrase; in other cases, it can be best conveyed by means of an admittedly imperfect and open-ended definition of the proto-type.

Linguists are conditioned by their training to start talking, at this point, about the difference between genuinely linguistic knowledge and knowledge of the world, about the difference between the ideal mental lexicon and an encyclopedia, about the difference between competence and performance, about the difference between semantics and pragmatics. None of these dichotomies is without value; but they are not to be identified with one another; and none of them can be drawn sharply in all cases.

It should now be pointed out that the term 'natural kind' and my presentation of the topic so far, is misleading in one respect. In view of the traditional associations of 'natural kind' and its philosophical underpinnings in current discussion, words denoting natural kinds in the traditional sense might be thought to differ semantically from words denoting what I will call *cultural kinds*, like 'dirt' or 'chair'. There is no reason to believe that they do. We have proto-types of the one as we have of the other, and we give the same kind of open-ended definitions combining both phenomenal and functional criteria. In fact, natural kinds in the traditional sense are often combined and divided by languages, in just the way that structuralists have suggested, sometimes arbitrarily, but often for culturally explicable reasons. For example, 'fruit' and 'vegetable' each cover several natural kinds, and in their most common, everyday, sense are fuzzy and indeterminate. Insofar as their denotation is clear in their proto-typical, or focal, sense the principal criterion which serves to classify a particular natural kind as being either a fruit or a vegetable is culinary: whether it is eaten, in English-speaking communities, as part of a main meal with meat or fish; whether it is used to make soup; and so on. The truth of the matter seems to be that the cultural and the natural are so intimately associated in the vocabularies of human languages that it often impossible to say, in most cases, that the one is more basic than the other, in either of the two senses of 'basic' discussed in the preceding section.

This fact emerges very clearly from research that has been carried out on a wide variety of languages, in selected areas of the vocabulary, by anthropologists, psychologists and linguists. Much of this research has been inspired, in recent years, by the important and seminal work on the vocabulary of colour by Berlin and

Kay (1969). Other areas of vocabulary – or *lexical fields* – that have been investigated from the same point of view include those of shape, botanical and biological nomenclature, and cooking. In general reviews of this work it is customary for authors to emphasize the cross-cultural validity of certain focal categories. It is no less important, however, to insist upon the fact that there is also a good deal of culture-dependent variation across languages. What I said about the meaning of 'fruit' and 'vegetable' in the previous paragraph is typical of all lexical fields, including those of colour and shape. For example, the fact that 'red' and 'white' are used to distinguish two broad categories of wine is something that cannot be accounted for in terms of the focal meanings of these words. It is a culturally established convention, and one that must be learned as one learns to use 'red' and 'white' in a range of characteristic situations and characteristic collocations.

It must also be emphasized that the notion of focal and peripheral meaning applies equally to all areas of the vocabulary. Not only natural-kind terms, on the one hand, and cultural-kind terms, on the other, fall within its scope. So too do abstract terms, no less than words denoting entities and substances in the physical world. In short, there is no reason for the linguist to think that there is anything special, from a semantic point of view, about those words whose focal meaning is determined by the properties of the physical world and the perceptual mechanisms of human beings.

Summary

In this chapter, we have shown that finding a satisfactory definition for a word is considerably more difficult than it seems to be at first sight. In fact, we have come finally to the view that most everyday words – words denoting natural and cultural kinds – are necessarily somewhat indeterminate in meaning, and, therefore, for theoretically

interesting reasons, undefinable. We have also introduced the distinction between focal and peripheral
meaning, and the no less important distinction between
denotation and sense. In the next chapter, we shall be
concerned with two different approaches to the analysis of
lexical sense: componential analysis and the use of
meaning-postulates.

4 *Webs of Words*

The formalization of lexical structure

'. . . where every word is at home,
Taking its place to support the others.'
T.S. Eliot, *Little Gidding*

People often think of the meanings of words as if each of them had an independent and separate existence. But, as we saw in the last chapter, no word can be fully understood independently of other words that are related to it and delimit its sense. Looked at from a semantic point of view, the lexical structure of a language – the structure of its vocabulary – is best regarded as a large and intricate network of sense-relations: it is like a huge, multidimensional, spider's web, in which each strand is one such relation and each knot in the web is a different lexeme.

In this chapter we discuss two approaches to the problem of describing the lexical structure of languages in a precise and systematic way. We shall make use of a few simple notions borrowed from modern logic.

Componential analysis

One way of formalizing, or making absolutely precise, the sense-relations that hold among lexemes is by means of *componential analysis*. As the name implies, this involves the analysis of the sense of a lexeme into its component parts. It has a long history in philosophical discussions of language. But it is only recently that it has been employed at all extensively by linguists. An alternative term for componential analysis is *lexical decomposition*.

Let us begin with a much used example. The words 'boy', 'girl', 'man' and 'woman' all denote human beings. We can therefore extract from the sense of each of them the common factor "human": i.e., the sense of the English word 'human'. Similarly, we can extract from "boy" and "man" the common factor "male", and from "girl" and "woman", the common factor "female". As for "man" and "woman", they can be said to have as one of their factors the *sense-component* "adult", in contrast with "boy" and "girl", which lack "adult" or, to be more precise, contain "non-adult". The sense of each of the four words can thus be represented as the product of three factors:

$$\text{"man"} = \text{"human"} \times \text{"male"} \times \text{"adult"}$$
$$\text{"woman"} = \text{"human"} \times \text{"female"} \times \text{"adult"}$$
$$\text{"boy"} = \text{"human"} \times \text{"male"} \times \text{"non-adult"}$$
$$\text{"girl"} = \text{"human"} \times \text{"female"} \times \text{"non-adult"}$$

I have deliberately used the multiplication-sign to emphasize the fact that these are intended to be taken as mathematically precise equations, to which the terms 'product' and 'factor' apply exactly as they do in, say, $30 = 2 \times 3 \times 5$. So far so good. Whether the equations we set up are empirically correct is another matter. We shall come to this.

Actually, sense-components are not generally represented by linguists in the way that I have introduced them. Instead of saying that "man" is the product of "human", "male" and "adult", it is more usual to identify its factors as HUMAN, MALE and ADULT. This is not simply a matter of typographical preference. By convention, small capitals are employed to refer to the allegedly universal sense-components out of which the senses of expressions in particular natural languages are constructed. Much of the attraction of componential analysis derives from the possibility of identifying such universal sense-components in the lexical structure of different languages. They are frequently described as basic atomic concepts – in the sense of 'basic' that is dominant in the philosophical tradition, which, as was noted in Chapter 3, does not necessarily correspond with the other, more obvious, sense of 'basic'.

What, then, is the relation between HUMAN and "human", between MALE and "male", and so on? This theoretically important question is not even raised in most presentations. It is simply assumed that "male" means MALE: that MALE is identical with "male". It is only on this assumption (in default of the provision of more explicit rules of interpretation) that the decomposition of "man" into MALE, ADULT and HUMAN can be interpreted as saying anything about the sense-relations that hold among the English words 'man', 'male', 'human' and 'adult'. We shall, therefore, make the assumption. This leaves open the obvious question (which I will not attempt to answer and the reader may treat as rhetorical): why should English, or any other natural language, have privileged status as a metalanguage for the semantic analysis of all languages?

We can now develop the formalization a little further. First of all, we can abstract the negative component from "non-adult" and replace it with the *negation-operator*, as this is defined in standard propositional logic: '$\sim$'. (Alternatively, and in effect equivalently, we can distinguish a positive and negative value of the two-valued variable $\pm$ADULT: viz. $+$ADULT and $-$ADULT. Linguists working within the framework of Chomskyan generative grammar have normally made use of this second type of notation.) We now have as a basic, presumably atomic, component ADULT, together with its complementary $\sim$ADULT. If MALE and FEMALE are also complementary, we can take one of them as basic and form the other from it by means of the same negation-operator.

But which of them is more basic, either in nature or in

culture, than the other? The question is of considerable theoretical interest if we are seriously concerned with establishing an inventory of universal sense-components. It is in principle conceivable that there is no universally valid answer. What is fairly clear, however, is that, as far as the vocabulary of English is concerned, it is normally MALE that one wants to treat as being more general and thus, in one sense, more basic. Feminists might argue, and perhaps rightly, that this fact is culturally explicable. At any rate, there are culturally explicable exceptions: 'nurse', 'secretary', etc., among words that (normally) denote human beings; 'goose', 'duck', and in certain respects 'cow', among words denoting domesticated animals. As for HUMAN, this is in contrast with a whole set of what from one point of view are equally basic components: let us call them CANINE, FELINE, BOVINE etc. They are equally basic in that they can be thought of as denoting the complex defining properties of natural kinds.

Earlier, I used the multiplication-sign to symbolize the operation by means of which components are combined. Let me now substitute for this the propositional connective of *conjunction*: '&'. We can then rewrite the analysis of "man", "woman", "boy", "girl" as:

"man"   = HUMAN & MALE & ADULT
"woman" = HUMAN & ~MALE & ADULT
"boy"   = HUMAN & MALE & ~ADULT
"girl" = HUMAN & ~MALE & ~ADULT

And to this we may add:

"child" = HUMAN & ~ADULT

in order to make clear the difference between the absence of a component and its negation. The absence of ~MALE from the representation of the sense of 'child' differentiates "child" from "girl". As for 'horse', 'stallion', 'mare', 'foal', 'sheep', 'ram', 'ewe', 'lamb', 'bull', 'cow', 'calf' – these, and many other sets of words, can be analysed in the same way by substituting EQUINE, OVINE, BOVINE, etc., as the case may be, for HUMAN.

The only logical operations utilized so far are negation and conjunction. Actually, in using symbols for propositional operators, '$\sim$' and '&', and attaching them directly, not to propositions, but to what logicians would call predicates, I have taken for granted a good deal of additional formal apparatus. Some of this will be introduced later. The formalization that I have employed is not the only possible one. I might equally well have used, at this point, the terminology and notation of elementary *set theory*, as it is taught almost universally nowadays in primary school. Everything said so far about the compositional nature of lexical meaning could be expressed in terms of sets and their complements and of the intersection of sets. For example, "boy" = HUMAN & MALE & $\sim$ADULT can be construed as telling us that any element that falls within the extension of the word 'boy' is contained in the intersection of three sets H, M and A', where H is the extension of 'human' (whose intension is HUMAN = "human"), M is the extension of 'male' and A' is the complement of the extension of 'adult'. This is illustrated graphically by means of so-called Venn diagrams (which will be familiar to many) in Figure 2.

There are several reasons for introducing these elementary notions of set theory at this point. First, they

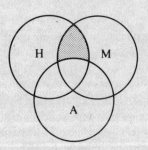

Fig. 2: The shaded portion represents the intersection of H, M and A'.

are implicit, though rarely made explicit, in the more informal presentations of componential analysis by linguists, anthropologists and psychologists. Second, they are well understood and have been precisely formulated in modern mathematical logic; and as we shall see in Part 2, they play an important role in the most influential systems of formal semantics. Finally, they enable us to give a very precise interpretation to the term 'product' when we say that the sense of a lexeme is the product of its components, or factors. More generally, we can say that the sense of a lexeme (or one of its senses) is a *compositional function* of its sense-components: i.e., its value is fully determined by (i) the value of the components and (ii) the definition of the operations by means of which they are combined. To say that the sense of a lexeme is a set-theoretic function of its sense-components is to say that it is a compositional function of a particularly simple kind. The notion of *compositionality*, as we shall see in Part 3, is absolutely central in all modern formal semantics. So too is the mathematical sense of the term 'function'. Anyone who has mastered the rudiments of elementary set theory at school (or indeed of simple arithmetic and algebra considered from a sufficiently general point of view) will be familiar with the principle of compositionality already, though he may never have met the actual terms 'compositionality' and 'function' until now.

The words used so far to illustrate the principles of componential analysis can be seen as property-denoting words. They are comparable with what logicians call one-place predicates: expressions which have one place to be filled, as it were, in order for them to be used in a well-formed proposition. For example, if 'John' is associated with the one-place predicate 'boy', the result is a simple sentence which expresses the proposition "John is a boy". (For simplicity, I have omitted many details that will occupy us later.) Other words, notably transitive verbs (e.g., 'hit', 'kill'), most prepositions, and nouns like 'father', 'mother', etc. denote two-place relations: they denote the relation that holds between the two entities referred to by the expressions that fill the two places. This means that their decomposition must take account of the directionality of the relations. For example,

$$\text{"father"} = \text{PARENT \& MALE}$$

is inadequate in that it leaves unrepresented the directionality of the relation of fatherhood. It may be expanded by adding *variables* in the appropriate places:

$$\text{"father"} = (X, Y)\text{PARENT \& } (X)\text{MALE,}$$

which expresses the fact that X is the parent of Y and X is male. This not only makes clear the directionality of the relations. It also tells us that it is the sex of X, not of Y, that is relevant.

There are other complications. Most important of all is the necessity of introducing in the representation of the sense of certain lexemes a hierarchical structure which reflects the syntactic structure of sentences. For example, "give" is more or less plausibly analysed as one two-place structure $(Y, Z)\text{HAVE}$, within another $(X,)\text{CAUSE}$:

$$(X, (Y, Z) \text{ HAVE}) \text{ CAUSE,}$$

which may be read as meaning – the question of tense may be left on one side – "X causes Y to have Z". And "kill", similarly, as a one-place structure within the same two-place structure:

$$(X, (Y) \text{ DIE}) \text{ CAUSE,}$$

which may be read as meaning "X causes Y to die". Representations of this kind presuppose a much more powerful system of formalization than the set-theoretic operations sufficient, in principle, for the examples used earlier in this section. Nevertheless, there is no doubt that the compositionality of more complex examples like "give" and "kill" can be formalized. Several somewhat different proposals have been made in recent years, notably by linguists subscribing to the tenets of generative semantics.

The empirical basis for componential analysis

To say that componential analysis can be formalized is quite a different matter from saying that it is theoretically interesting or in conformity with the facts as they present themselves to us in real life. In other words, theoretical motivation and empirical validity raise questions of a different order from those relating to formalization. Componential analysis is no longer defended by linguists, on theoretical grounds, as enthusiastically as it was by many a few years ago. Some of the reasons for this change of heart have to do with more general issues pertaining to any allegedly exhaustive and determinate analysis of the sense of lexemes. Others relate more specifically to componential analysis as such.

The theoretical motivation for componential analysis is clear enough. It provides us, in principle, with a systematic and economical means of representing the sense-relations that hold among lexemes in particular languages and, on the assumption that the components are universal, across languages. But much of this theoretical motivation is undermined when one looks more carefully at particular analyses. First of all, there is the problem of deciding which of the two senses of 'basic' discussed in the previous chapter should determine the selection of the putative atomic universal components. There is no reason to believe that what is basic in the sense of being maximally general is also basic in the day-to-day thinking of most users of a language. Furthermore, it can be demonstrated that, if we always extract those components that can be identified in the largest number of lexemes, we shall frequently end up with a less economical and less systematic analysis for particular lexemes than we would do if we analysed each lexeme on its own terms.

As for the empirical validity of componential analysis, it is not difficult to show that this is more apparent than real. For example, the analysis of "boy", "girl" and "child" given above tells us that all boys and all girls are children. But this is not true: we cannot legitimately infer from the proposition "John is a boy and Jane is a girl" the proposition "John and Jane are children" (in the relevant sense of 'child'). And there is no point in saying that this is a matter of the use, rather than the meaning, of 'child'. The English expressions 'male child' and 'female child' are not synonymous with 'boy' and 'girl'. At the very least, therefore, something must be added to the analysis to capture this fact. And what about the analysis of the sense of 'boy' and 'girl' in relation to that of 'man' and 'woman'? Even here ~ADULT creates difficulty. First of all, neither the proposition "That boy is now an adult" nor "That girl is now an adult" (unlike "That child is now an adult") appear to be in any way anomalous. How, then, in this case, does ADULT relate to "adult"? Second, there is the fact that, in most contexts, 'girl' and 'woman' are not used as contradictories, whereas 'boy' and 'man', though they may not be contradictories in the strict sense, are certainly more sharply opposed to one another semantically than 'girl' and 'woman' are. Finally, none of the more obvious and relatively objective criteria of adulthood – sexual maturity, legal majority, economic and social independence, etc. – is relevant, except in certain contexts, to the use, descriptively, of 'man' rather than 'boy' or of 'woman' rather than 'girl'. Needless to say, these difficulties are compounded when we start comparing the analysis of 'child' with that of 'lamb' or 'foal' – not to mention that of 'boy' and 'girl' with that of 'colt' and 'filly'!

Similarly, it can be argued that, although HUMAN is an essential component of "man" and "woman", it is not an essential component of "boy", and possibly not of "girl".

The male offspring of the gods (e.g., Cupid) are regularly described as boys (and their female offspring, in the appropriate circumstances, as maidens); but they do not grow up to be men, and they are not said to be human. This is not a facetious point. There is a tendency for tough-minded, uncompromising theoreticians to say that, in cases like this, 'boy' is not being used with its literal meaning. But this is surely wrong. We must be careful not to import our own metaphysical prejudices into the analysis of the vocabularies of natural languages. Still less must we make the distinction between literal and non-literal meaning dependent upon them.

If componential analysis is defective both theoretically and empirically, why have I devoted so much space to it? Partly, because it has figured prominently in recent works on semantics and guided a good deal of research. Partly, also, because there is another way of looking at componential analysis which makes it less obviously defective. This is to take it, not as a technique for the representation of all and only the meaning of lexemes, but as a way of formalizing that part of their *proto-typical*, or focal, meaning which they share with other lexemes. For example, there is no doubt that 'boy' is used proto-typically of human beings and furthermore that, insofar as we understand it when it is used descriptively of Cupid, we do so because we understand it, first of all, in relation to human beings. So HUMAN is criterial for the focal meaning of 'boy' and serves also, analogically, in non-focal uses. But it is not part of its intension: i.e., of the property which defines the class whose members it denotes. Most of the allegedly universal components that have been proposed are of this kind.

Entailment and possible worlds

Entailment plays an important role in all theories of meaning, and a more central role in some than in others. Take the following two propositions, which I have labelled p and q (for reasons that will be explained immediately):

> "Achilles killed Hector"   (p)
>
> "Hector died"   (q)

Here the first proposition, p, necessarily implies, or *entails*, the second proposition, q: if it is the case that Achilles killed Hector, then it is necessarily the case that Hector died. In logical terminology entailment is a relation that holds between p and q – where p and q are variables standing for propositions – such that, if the truth of q necessarily follows from the truth of p (and the falsity of q necessarily follows from the falsity of p), then p entails q. The key term here is 'necessarily'.

It should be noted that entailment has been defined as a relation between *propositions*. This is important. Some authors talk of entailments as holding between sentences. In doing so, they are using the term 'sentence' either loosely or in a very special sense. Others, for reasons that we need not go into here, define entailment as a relation between statements. But this usage, too, rests upon a specialized interpretation of 'statement', which conflicts in several respects with its everyday sense in English and can lead to confusion. I will discuss the relation between sentences and propositions in Part 3, and the nature of statements, as well as that of questions, commands etc. in Part 4. At this point, I would simply draw the reader's attention to the fact that I have now extended my use of double quotation-marks to cover propositions.

There is no standard symbolization of the relation of entailment. I will use a double-shafted arrow. Thus

$$p \Rightarrow q$$

will mean "p entails q". The logical relation thus symbolized can be defined, in modal logic, in terms of implication and necessity. We need not go into the formalism. But we do need to discuss the notion of necessity itself in rather more detail than is customary in linguistics and the social sciences.

Propositions may be either necessarily or contingently true (or false). A necessarily true (or false) proposition is one that is true (or false) in all possible circumstances: as Leibniz put it, *in all possible worlds*. For example, the propositions "Snow is white" and "Rabbits are human" might well be necessarily true and necessarily false, respectively. A contingently true (or false) proposition, on the other hand, is one whose truth-value might have been, or might be, different in other circumstances. For example,

"Napoleon was defeated at Waterloo"
is contingent in the required sense. We can envisage a possible world, or a possible state of the world, of which it is not true. This intuitively comprehensible notion of *possible worlds* (satirized, incidentally, in its theological development by Leibniz in Voltaire's *Candide*) has been formalized in various ways in modern modal logic. For logical purposes, a possible world may be identified with the set of propositions that truly describe it. It is under this interpretation of 'world' that one talks of propositions being true in, rather than of, a world. It will be noted that I have used both ways of talking about worlds in this paragraph.

So far, so good! Problems emerge as soon as we start examining the notion of necessity more closely. Two sub-types of necessary truths are recognized by philosophers: analytic and logical. They are frequently confused in general treatments by linguists. It is important to draw the distinction clearly. According to Kant, a proposition is *analytically* true if the meaning of the subject is contained in that of the predicate. A reasonably uncontroversial, and by now traditional, example is

"All bachelors are unmarried",
on the assumption that 'bachelor' is taken in the appropriate sense (and not as meaning "someone who has acquired his first university degree", etc.). Let us call the

sense in question "bachelor$_1$". Granted that "unmarried" is contained in "bachelor$_1$", the truth of "All bachelors are unmarried" can be demonstrated by analysis of the subject-expression, 'all bachelors', and more especially of 'bachelor'. The sense of 'bachelor' (i.e., "bachelor$_1$") can be analysed, or decomposed, into "unmarried" (or possibly "never married") and "man". So the proposition we are discussing is equivalent to

"All unmarried men are unmarried"

in which the predicate "unmarried" is patently contained in the subject. One can see immediately both the original motivation for the use of the term 'analytic' and the relevance, to this topic, of the technique of componential analysis. Nowadays, it is more common to reformulate the definition of analyticity in more general terms: an analytically true (or false) proposition is one whose truth-value is determined solely by its meaning. This is the formulation that we shall adopt. Any proposition that is not analytic is, by definition, *synthetic*. Therefore, all contingent propositions, such as "Napoleon was defeated at Waterloo", are synthetic. It does not follow, however, that all synthetic propositions are contingent. I will not develop this point, though it is important and has been much discussed by philosophers.

We come now to the question of logical truth. A *logically* true (or false) proposition is one whose truth-value is determined solely by the *logical form* of the proposition: e.g., "All unmarried men are unmarried". What is meant by 'logical form' is, in part, controversial. Even more controversial is the relation between the logical form of propositions and the structure of natural-language sentences. But I will simply assume that 'logical form' is satisfactorily defined in standard systems of logic and that, in straightforward cases at least, we have an intuitive understanding of it. I am assuming, for example, that "All unmarried men are unmarried", "All red books are red", etc., are recognized intuitively as logical truths. They would certainly be so classified, by virtue of their form, in all standard systems of logic. As I have said earlier, logical truths constitute one of two sub-types of necessary truths. Furthermore, if logical form is held to be a part of the meaning of propositions, logical truths are a sub-class of analytic truths. All this follows by definition. It has been argued that all analytic truths are also logical truths; but this is highly controversial and cannot be taken for granted. It has also been argued, or simply assumed without argument, that the only necessary truths are logical truths. In my view, there are very good reasons for recognizing different kinds, not only of non-logical necessity, but also of non-analytic necessity.

Linguists have often used the term 'necessarily', and even 'entailment', rather loosely. Insofar as they are concerned with the semantic structure of natural languages, it is not necessarily true propositions as such that should be of interest to them, but analytically true propositions (including logical truths as a sub-type). Similarly, if entailment is defined as above, it is not entailment in its entirety that is, or should be, of central concern, but rather what might be called semantic, or analytic, entailment. Generally speaking, this is what linguists seem to have in mind. Henceforth I shall use the term 'entailment' in this narrower sense. It is of course possible to argue that all necessary truths are analytic, as I indicated earlier. On the face of it, however, this is patently not the case.

First of all, there are propositions which, if true, are true by virtue of natural, or physical, necessity: i.e., by virtue of the laws of nature. (The qualification, "if true", is important. We must never confuse the epistemological status of a proposition with its truth-value.) One such proposition might be:

"All men are mortal."

Arguably this proposition, if true, is true by virtue of biological necessity (which, according to current conceptions, is a particular kind of natural necessity). And yet it is surely not analytic. The meaning of 'man' would not suddenly change if it were discovered, contrary to popular belief and so far well-established scientific hypotheses, that some men are immortal.

Once we have seen the distinction between natural necessity and necessity by virtue of meaning in a fairly obvious case like the one above, it is easier to appreciate that many examples of entailment that figure in the recent literature are dubious, to say the least, if it is the narrower sense of 'entailment' that is involved. What about the following, for instance?

"Jackie is pregnant" ⇒ "Jackie is female"

At first sight, one might be inclined to say that this is true by virtue of the meaning of 'pregnant' and 'female'. A moment's reflection, however, will show that we are not dealing with a valid example of semantic entailment. Let us suppose that advances in surgical and immunological techniques made it possible to transplant into a man a foetus-bearing womb (and everything else that the hypothesis requires) and then to deliver the child by Caesarean section. One can think of several variations on this theme, all of which, simply by being conceptually coherent, cast doubt upon the view that "female" is part of the meaning of 'pregnant'. But we do not have to speculate about the details. It suffices that we are able to discuss rationally the possibility of a man being pregnant and argue about the personal and social consequences. If we impose upon 'possible world' the same restrictions as we have imposed upon 'entailment', we can say that there are possible worlds in which "X is pregnant" does not entail "Y is female" (where 'X' and 'Y' stand for any appropriate expressions). After all, as Leibniz might have said, God could have ordained things differently in some world other than the best of all possible worlds, which, in his wisdom, he has actualized!

As we have recognized cultural kinds, in addition to natural kinds, so we might recognize cultural necessity, in addition to natural necessity. For example, it is arguably a matter of cultural necessity, in our culture, that marriage should be a symmetrical relation between two persons of different sex. This being so, provided that we are using English to talk about a culture in which the same conditions hold true (in relation to cohabitation, social and economic roles, etc.), we could say that "X is married to Y" necessarily implies "Y is married to X"; that the conjunction of "X is male" and "X is married to Y" necessarily implies "Y is female", etc. This is obviously different from natural necessity. Furthermore, it is easy to envisage other cultures in which homosexual unions (involving cohabitation, etc.), are not only accepted, but regulated by law and religion on the same footing as heterosexual unions. One can envisage, without much difficulty, trilateral unions, in which each member is correctly described, regardless of his or her biological sex, as the wife of one and the husband of another. Or again, we can easily imagine amendments to our own divorce laws such that it becomes possible for one partner's marital status to be changed without consequential and reciprocal changes in the status of the other. In such circumstances "X is married to Y" would no longer necessarily imply "Y is married to X". Arguably, however, the meaning of 'married' would not have changed.

At the very least, the consideration of possibilities like this makes us realize that semantic entailment is by no means as clear-cut as it is often held to be. We do not have to go all the way with such philosophers as Quine in their criticism of the analytic/synthetic distinction. But we must certainly agree with him when he says that the distinction, as far as natural languages are concerned, is not sharp. I will not press the point further. But I would encourage the reader to look critically at what are alleged to be entailments in recent works in theoretical semantics. Many of them are certainly not entailments, and others are of doubtful status with respect to analyticity.

Sense-relations and meaning postulates

In Chapter 3, a distinction was drawn between denotation and sense, and sense was defined in terms of *sense-relations*. Some of them were exemplified, but without discussion. None of them, apart from descriptive synonymy, has yet been named or defined. Since I have dealt with the nature of sense-relations at some length in other publications, I will give the briefest possible outline here. My principal concern in the present context is to show how sense-relations of various kinds can be formalized.

Sense-relations are of two kinds: *substitutional* and *combinatorial* (or, in the Saussurean terms more familiar to linguists, paradigmatic and syntagmatic). Substitutional relations are those which hold between inter-substitutable members of the same category; combinatorial relations hold typically, though not necessarily, between expressions of different categories (e.g., between nouns and adjectives, between verbs and adverbs, etc.). For example, a substitutional relation (of a particular kind) holds between the nouns 'bachelor' and 'spinster', whereas the relation that holds between the adjective 'unmarried' and the nouns 'man' and 'woman' is combinatorial. The lexically composite expressions 'unmarried man' and 'unmarried woman' are not only syntactically well-formed, but by virtue of the *congruity* of the sense of the adjective with the sense of both of the nouns they are also *collocationally* acceptable: that is, they can occur together in the same construction. It is intuitively obvious, on the basis of these and other examples, that a more specific, lexically and syntactically simpler, expression may be descriptively equivalent to a lexically composite expression in which two (or several) more general expressions are combined. For example, 'foal' may be descriptively equivalent to 'baby horse'.

I shall have little to say here about combinatorial sense-relations, since they bring us into the area of grammatical meaning and sentence semantics. It is important to note that certain lexemes are so highly restricted with respect to collocational acceptability that it is impossible to predict their combinatorial relations on the basis of an independent characterization of their sense. Classic examples from English are the adjectives 'rancid' and 'addled'. It is clearly an important part of knowing their sense to know that 'rancid' combines, or collocates, with 'butter', and 'addled' with 'egg' (and, metaphorically, with 'brain'). The view taken here is that the sense of any lexeme, whether it is highly restricted with respect to collocational acceptability or not, includes both its combinatorial and its substitutional relations.

Substitutional relations of sense, insofar as they will be dealt with here, are also of two kinds: hyponymy and incompatibility. They are both definable in terms of entailment.

The relation of *hyponymy* is exemplified by such pairs of expressions as 'dog' and 'animal', of which the former is a hyponym of the latter: the sense of 'dog' includes that of 'animal'. Entailment, as we saw in the previous section, is a relation that holds between propositions. However, provided that we keep this fact in mind, it is convenient to be able to say, in a kind of shorthand, that one word or phrase entails another. Adopting this kind of shorthand we can say one expression, f, is a hyponym of another expression, g, if and only if f entails g: i.e.,

$$f \Rightarrow g.$$

For example, 'dog' entails 'animal'. Given a proposition p containing 'dog', the substitution of 'animal' for 'dog' in p will yield another proposition q which is entailed by p. Thus:

"I saw a dog"   (p)

entails

"I saw an animal"   (q).

In this case no syntactic adjustments need to be made. We still have to relate propositions to utterances (and propositional content to sentences). If this can be done, the statement that 'dog' is a hyponym of 'animal' can be given a precise formal interpretation. All this will be of concern to us later. But what is the status of $f \Rightarrow g$ from a formal point of view?

It is best construed as what logicians, following Carnap, call a *meaning postulate*. Generally speaking, the use of meaning postulates has been seen by linguists as an alternative to componential analysis. Looked at from this point of view, the advantage of meaning postulates over componential analysis is that they do not presuppose the exhaustive decomposition of the sense of a lexeme into an integral number of universal sense-components. They can be defined for lexemes as such, without making any assumptions about atomic concepts, and they can be used to give a partial account of the sense of a lexeme without the necessity of providing a total analysis. From an empirical point of view these are very considerable advantages.

Of course, the validity of any particular meaning postulate, such as

'dog' $\Rightarrow$ 'animal'

for English will depend upon whether the alleged entailment is in fact analytic. In this connection, it is worth noting the possibility of ordering the meaning-postulates associated with a particular lexeme hierarchically in terms of their degree of analyticity. For example,

'bachelor' $\Rightarrow$ 'unmarried'

seems to be more highly, or more definitely, analytic than

'bachelor' $\Rightarrow$ 'adult'

and perhaps also than

$$\text{‘bachelor’} \Rightarrow \text{‘man’}.$$

Let us suppose, for example, that child-marriages were legalized and became a matter of everyday occurrence in some English-speaking society. One would presumably not hesitate to use the word ‘bachelor’ of an unmarried child in such circumstances. And, arguably, there would have been no change in the sense of ‘bachelor’. It is far more difficult to envisage comparable circumstances in which ‘bachelor’ $\Rightarrow$ ‘unmarried’ is invalidated without some other associated change in the sense of either ‘bachelor’ or ‘unmarried’. Regardless of the empirical status of the particular example, it is clear, therefore, that speakers of a language may regard some entailments of a word as more central or more determinate than other entailments of the same word. Hierarchically ordered meaning postulates can be used to capture the indeterminacy of the boundary between the analytic and the synthetic. I have made this point in relation to hyponymy, but it holds for all the sense-relations that can be formalized in terms of meaning postulates.

Before we continue, it is worth noting that descriptive synonymy may be defined in terms of symmetrical hyponymy. Although the term ‘hyponymy’ is customarily used for an asymmetrical relation of entailment (i.e., where $f \Rightarrow g$, but not $g \Rightarrow f$: ‘dog’ $\Rightarrow$ ‘animal’ is true, whereas ‘animal’ $\Rightarrow$ ‘dog’ is false), there is nothing in the formal definition of hyponymy which makes this essential. Using a double-headed, double-shafted arrow to symbolize symmetrical entailment, we can say that

$$f \Leftrightarrow g$$

establishes the descriptive synonymy of f and g (e.g., ‘puppy’ $\Leftrightarrow$ ‘baby dog’). It can be readily proved that the definition of descriptive synonymy in terms of symmetrical entailment is equivalent to the following: two expressions are descriptively synonymous if and only if they have the same entailments.

The second kind of substitutional sense-relation is *incompatibility* which is definable in terms of entailment and negation:

$$f \Rightarrow \sim g \quad \text{and} \quad g \Rightarrow \sim f.$$

For example, 'red' and 'blue' are defined to be incompatible in this way: if something is red it is necessarily not blue, and conversely. A special case of incompatibility is *complementarity*, when, in addition to the above, the following conditions are also satisfied:

$$\sim f \Rightarrow g \quad \text{and} \quad \sim g \Rightarrow f.$$

For example, not only does 'married' entail the negation of 'unmarried' (and conversely), but the negation of 'unmarried' entails 'married'. Complementarity is often treated as a kind of antonymy ("oppositeness of meaning").

But *antonymy* in the narrowest sense – polar antonymy – differs from complementarity in virtue of gradability. This means that the conjunction of two negated antonyms is not contradictory. For example, 'good' and 'bad' are polar antonyms, and "X is neither good nor bad" is perfectly acceptable, even though "X is not good" might be held to imply "X is bad" (in some looser sense of 'imply') in many contexts. When they are graded in an explicitly comparative construction ("X is better than Y"), the following holds:

$$f^+(x, y) \Leftrightarrow g^+(y, x),$$

where the superscript plus-sign is a non-standard, but convenient, way of symbolizing "more". For example, if f is 'good' and g is 'bad', then f^+ and g^+ symbolize the selection of the forms *better* and *worse* ("more good" and "more bad"). If we substitute expressions referring to particular individuals for x and y, we see that, for example, "John is better than Peter" entails and is entailed by "Peter is worse than John".

In fact, expressions with the meanings "more good" and "more bad" are two-term *converses*. They are like corresponding active and passive verb-expresssions ('kill': 'be killed'), and also like such pairs of lexemes as 'husband': 'wife' (due allowance being made in both cases for the associated syntactic adjustments). The verbs 'buy' and 'sell' exemplify the class of three-term lexical converses:

$$\text{'buy' } (x, y, z) \Rightarrow \text{'sell' } (z, y, x).$$

For example, "Mary (x) bought the car (y) from Paul (z)" entails, and is entailed by, "Paul (z) sold the car (y) to Mary (x)". Obviously, what I have here called syntactic adjustments (to avoid the more specific implications of the term 'transformation' in linguistics) need to be precisely specified. Provided that this is done and that we can give a satisfactory account of the relation between sentences, propositions and utterances, we can account formally for sets of entailments like "John killed Peter" $\Rightarrow$ "Peter was killed by John", "Mary is John's wife" $\Rightarrow$ "John is Mary's husband", "John bought a car from Peter" $\Rightarrow$ "Peter sold John a car", and so on.

This is a big proviso! Before we address ourselves to it in Parts 3 and 4, it is worth emphasizing the fact that in this chapter we have been concerned solely with the descriptive meaning of expressions. Furthermore, limitations of space have allowed me to mention only the most important of the relations that hold, by virtue of sense, in the vocabularies of natural languages. My main concern has been to give the reader some idea of what is involved in the formalization of lexical structure and to outline two alternatives that linguists have pursued in recent years. There is perhaps no reason, in principle, why the non-descriptive meaning of lexemes should not also be formalizable. But so far at least formal semantics has taken the same limited view of lexical structure as I have done here.

Summary

In this chapter, I have outlined a number of the most important sense-relations that exist in the vocabularies of natural languages, and I have explained two of the ways in which linguists have tried to formalize them in recent years. As I have indicated, componential analysis looks far less promising than methods of analysis based on the notion of meaning postulates.

Our discussion of lexical structure has familiarized us with some logical concepts which will be useful for the treatment of sentence-meaning and utterance-meaning in Parts 3 and 4. Indeed, it should by now be evident that the formalization of lexical structure in terms of the truth and falsity of propositions presupposes a satisfactory account of the way in which propositions are expressed in natural languages. We cannot give such an account, even in outline, without discussing the propositional content of sentences. As we shall see in Part 3, propositional content is one part of sentence-meaning. At this point, then, we must move on from words to sentences.

PART 3

Sentences

5 *Making Sense with Sentences*

Distinguishing meaningful
from meaningless sentences

'Most true it is that I have look'd on truth
Askance and strangely.'
William Shakespeare, *Sonnets*

In general, we produce utterances such as
>   *Bill likes daffodils*
>   *Do you want another cup of tea?*
rather than, say,
>   *Abstractness swallowed a pale black week*
which, everyone would agree, is meaningless.
But what grounds do we have for drawing a theoretical
distinction between meaningful and meaningless sentences? The problem is more complex than many people
realize; this will become clear in the course of this
chapter. As we shall see, a number of linguists in recent
years have followed the philosophers and based their
account of sentence-meaning upon what are called truth-
conditions. We shall try to make clear how this particular
approach arose – an approach which has dominated all
others in recent years.

Grammaticality and meaningfulness

Sentences are, by definition, grammatically well-formed.
There is no such thing, therefore, as an ungrammatical
sentence. Many of the utterances that are produced in
normal everyday circumstances are ungrammatical in
various ways. Some of these are interpretable in the
context in which they occur. Indeed, they might well be
regarded by most speakers of the language as fully

acceptable. As we saw in Chapter 1, grammaticality must not be identified with acceptability.

However, at this point we will restrict our attention to what would generally be regarded as sentences and we will continue to operate with the assumption that the sentences of a language are readily identifiable as such by those who are competent in it, and more especially by its native speakers. As we shall see in due course, this assumption must be qualified. The distinction between grammatical and semantic well-formedness is not as sharp as, for the moment, we are taking it to be. Nevertheless, to say that the distinction between grammar and semantics is not clear-cut in all instances is not to say that it is never clear-cut at all.

There are many utterances whose unacceptability is quite definitely a matter of grammar, rather than semantics. For example,

> *I want that he will come*,

is definitely ungrammatical in Standard English in contrast with

> *I want him to come.*

If *I want that he will come* were produced by a foreigner, it would probably be construed, and therefore understood, as an incorrect version of *I want him to come*. There is nothing in what appears to be the intended meaning that makes it ungrammatical.

If someone, having uttered *I want that he will come*, not only refused the proffered correction, but insisted that it meant something different from the corrected version, we should simply have to tell him that, as far as Standard English is concerned, he is wrong. We can classify his utterance, unhesitatingly, as ungrammatical.

There are other, actual or potential, utterances which we can classify, no less readily, as grammatical, but meaningless. Among them, we can list such famous examples as

> *Colourless green ideas sleep furiously,*
> *Quadruplicity drinks procrastination,*
> *Thursday is in bed with Friday.*

Of course, none of these is uninterpretable, if it is appropriately contextualized and the meaning of one or more of its constituent words is extended beyond its normal, or literal, meaning by means of such traditionally recognized principles as metaphor, metonymy or synechdoche. The fact that this can be done – and indeed has been done on several occasions to considerable effect – merely proves the point that is being made here. In order to assign an interpretation to *Colourless green ideas sleep furiously*, etc., we do not identify, and tacitly correct, some general rule or principle of the structure of English, as we did in the case of *I want that he will come*. We ourselves try to make sense of what, at first sight, does not of itself make sense on a literal interpretation of its constituent expressions. We shall need to look later at the question of literal interpretation. All that needs to be said here is that *Colourless green ideas sleep furiously*, etc., are grammatically well-formed and that, despite their grammaticality, they are literally meaningless: i.e., if the words they contain are construed literally, the sentences that contain them do not make sense.

As we shall see later, there is more to the meaningfulness of sentences than is covered by the everyday intuitive notion of making sense. However, that part of the meaning of sentences which can be explicated as the product of the senses of the constituent lexemes – the sense, or propositional content, of sentences – is what we are concerned with at this point. And this kind of meaningfulness or semantic well-formedness is readily distinguishable, in clear cases, from grammaticality.

Corrigibility and translatability

But what are the criteria other than the intuitive notion of making sense which lead us to decide that a sentence is or is not semantically well-formed? Actually, we have tacitly invoked the main criterion we need in the previous section: the criterion of *corrigibility*. Whereas *I want that he will come* can be corrected – by some speakers to *I want him to come* and by others perhaps to *I want for him to come* – without any change in what is assumed to be the intended meaning, *Colourless green ideas sleep furiously* cannot. In those instances in which the distinction between grammatical and semantic unacceptability can be clearly drawn, the former are corrigible and the latter are not.

Other kinds of unacceptability, some of which at first sight seem to be a matter of meaning, also fall within the scope of the notion of corrigibility. For example,

  My father died last night

might be corrected to, say,

  My father passed away last night

in a language-community (of the kind envisaged in Chapter 1) in which the use of 'die' is prohibited with expressions referring to members of one's own family. But the unacceptability of *My father died last night*, in such circumstances, is not such that we would say that it does not make sense. Its unacceptability is a matter of social, rather than descriptive, meaning. (And there are independent reasons for saying that, though corrigible, it is a fully grammatical sentence.) In other instances, as we shall see later, the situation is less clear-cut. But, interestingly enough, the criterion of corrigibility and incorrigibility is still relevant in that it shows the pre-theoretically indeterminate cases to be genuinely indeterminate.

Another criterion that is sometimes mentioned by linguists is *translatability*. This rests on the view that semantic, but not grammatical, distinctions can be matched across languages. However, as we shall see later, it is not clear that what is semantically unacceptable in some languages is semantically unacceptable in all languages. The criterion of translatability can supplement, but it does not supplant, our main criterion, that of corrigibility.

We turn now to a discussion of a famous and influential philosophical criterion of meaningfulness.

Verifiability and verificationism

The verificationist theory of meaning – verificationism, for short – was mentioned in Chapter 1. As its name suggests, it has to do with truth. It was originally associated with the philosophical movement known as logical positivism, initiated by members of the Vienna Circle in the period immediately preceding the Second World War. Although logical positivism, and with it verificationism, is all but dead, it has been of enormous importance in the development of modern philosophical semantics. On the one hand, many of its proponents – notably Carnap and Reichenbach – were active in the construction of systems for the analysis of language which have led, more or less directly, to the methods of modern formal semantics. On the other, the very excesses and defects of logical positivism forced its opponents, including Wittgenstein in his later work and the so-called ordinary-language philosophers, to make explicit some of their own assumptions about meaning. As Ryle (1951: 250) has said of verificationism: 'It has helped to reveal the important fact that we talk sense in lots of different ways, and we talk nonsense in lots of different ways.'

We shall not pursue Ryle's point at this stage. Instead, I will take one version of the famous *verifiability principle* and, in the next few sections, use this to introduce the notion of truth-conditions and other notions that will be of use to us later. The principle may be stated, initially and for our purposes, as follows: 'A sentence is factually significant to a given person if, and only if, he knows how to verify the proposition which it purports to express' (Ayer, 1946: 35). This formulation by Ayer, it will be noted, does not say that the meaning of either sentences or propositions is their method of verification. It simply provides a criterion of one particular kind of meaning – factual significance; it does not define meaning as such.

Even so, it raises a number of problems. The logical positivists wanted to say that all verification was ultimately a matter of observation. Yet, as Popper has pointed out, universal statements of the kind that scientists tend to make cannot, in principle, be verified, though they may be falsified, by means of observation. For example, the statement that all swans are white can be falsified by observing just a single instance of a black swan, but it can never be proved to be true on the basis of empirical investigation. Popper's point that falsifiability, rather than verifiability, is the hallmark of scientific hypotheses is now widely accepted (though it has its critics and requires to be formulated more carefully than it has been here).

Propositions and propositional content

Ayer's formulation draws upon (though it does not explain) the distinction between sentences and *propositions*. The nature of propositions is philosophically controversial. But those philosophers who accept that propositions differ, on the one hand, from sentences and, on the other, from statements, questions, commands, etc., will usually say that propositions

(i)   are either true or false;
(ii) may be known, believed or doubted;
(iii) may be asserted, denied or queried;
(iv) are held constant under translation from one language to another.

There are difficulties, as we shall see later, about reconciling all four of these different criteria: (ii) and (iii) seem to be in conflict as far as some natural languages are concerned; and (iv) makes dubious assumptions about intertranslatability.

   However, granted that propositions are defined to be the bearers of a determinate and unchanging truth-value, it is quite clear that they must be distinguished from sentences. For the same sentence can be used on one

occasion to say what is true and on another to say what is
false. And it is worth noting, in this connection, that even
sentences like

    'Napoleon was defeated at Waterloo in 1815'
can be used to assert a variety of true and false propositions. There are certain natural languages in which
personal names and place-names are in one-to-one correspondence with their bearers. But English is not one of
them. If 'Napoleon' happens to be the name of my dog
and I am referring to my dog when I utter the above
sentence, the proposition that I have asserted is presumably false. (I introduce the qualification 'presumably' to remind the reader that I am making certain
background assumptions that he and others may not
share. For example, I have tacitly ruled out the possibility
that Napoleon Bonaparte may have been reincarnated as
my dog. There is nothing in the structure of English that
commits us to the denial of such possibilities.) Philosophers and linguists frequently make the point that
sentences containing definite descriptions (for example,
'the wooden door') or, more obviously, personal pronouns ('I', 'you', etc.), demonstrative pronouns ('this',
'that') or demonstrative adverbs of place and time ('here',
'there', 'now', 'then') can be used to assert, deny or query
indefinitely many true or false propositions. All too often
they fail to add that this is also the case for sentences
containing proper names and dates. The vast majority of
sentences in the most familiar natural languages do not
have a determinate and constant truth-value. Each of
them can be correlated, on particular occasions of utterance, with one proposition rather than another.

  But what exactly is the relationship between sentences
and propositions? This is a difficult question; and the
answer that one will give to it depends in part upon one's
theory of meaning. It suffices for present purposes to note
that certain assumptions must be made, whether tacitly or
explicitly, by anyone who says of sentences that they
express propositions. Ayer, it will be noted, is more

circumspect, in the quotation given above. He talks of sentences as *purporting* to express propositions; and it is easy to see why. The purport of a document is the meaning that it conveys by virtue of its appearance, or face-value, and standard assumptions about the interpretation of the author's intentions. Sentences of whatever kind may be uttered, in various circumstances, without there being any question of the assertion or denial of a proposition. For instance, if I am asked to provide someone with an example of an English sentence in the past tense, I might comply with his request by uttering 'Napoleon was defeated at Waterloo in 1815'. It is quite clear that, in the circumstances envisaged, the sentence that I have uttered cannot be construed as saying anything about Napoleon (no matter who or what might be legitimately referred to by this name).

For this and other reasons, we cannot say that sentences as such express propositions. What we can do, however, is to interpret the phrase 'purport to express a proposition' in terms of the notion of characteristic use, as explained in Chapter 1. And this is what I will do throughout the next three chapters. I will assume that all declarative sentences belong to the class of sentences whose members are used, characteristically, to make statements (that is, to assert or deny particular propositions) and that they have this potential for use encoded in their grammatical structure as part of their purport or face-value; that all interrogative sentences have encoded in their grammatical structure their potential for querying particular propositions; and so on. Under this interpretation of the notion of purport, or face-value, we can exclude from consideration not only a variety of metalinguistic uses of sentences and expressions, but also what will be identified in Part 4 as their *performative* and *indirect* uses.

Sentence-meaning is intrinsically connected with utterance-meaning, but can be distinguished from it by virtue of the distinction between the characteristic use of a sentence (which need not be its most frequent or psychologically most salient use) and its use on particular occasions. I have emphasized the notion of the *use* of sentences at this point because the so-called use theory of meaning, associated with Wittgenstein, Austin, and others, developed out of and in reaction to verificationism. What I want to do in this book is to throw a bridge between a restricted version of the meaning-as-use theory and the truth-conditional theory of meaning, which also developed historically out of verificationism. It is essential to the fulfilment of this purpose that what is said here about the purport, or face-value, of a sentence and what is said in Part 4 about the intrinsic connection between sentence-meaning and utterance-meaning should be properly understood.

It is also important that a distinction should be drawn between the propositions expressed by a sentence on particular occasions of utterance and its propositional content. I will come to this presently. Strictly speaking, as we shall see, most sentences do not even purport to express propositions, but propositional content. Provided that this is understood, together with the point made earlier about the purported, or face-value, use of sentences, no confusion will arise if, occasionally and for brevity's sake, we say, as most authors do, that sentences express propositions.

Non-factual significance and emotivism

There is one final point that may be made in connection with Ayer's statement: 'A sentence is factually significant to a given person if, and only if, he knows how to verify the proposition that it purports to express.' This has to do with factual significance. It was by means of the verifiability principle that the logical positivists wanted to prescribe as meaningless, or nonsensical, such metaphysical and theological sentences as, let us say, 'Every thing must have a cause' or 'God is good'. But it was soon realized that the principle also ruled out what many of them held to be the philosophically more respectable sentences of ethics and aesthetics: such as 'Cannibalism is wrong' or 'Monet is better than Manet'. One way round this problem was to say that, although such sentences are not factually significant, they have another kind of meaning: an emotive, or expressive meaning.

Emotivism – the thesis that in making what appear to be factual statements in ethics and aesthetics one is not saying anything that is true or false, but giving vent to one's feelings – has now, like logical positivism itself, been abandoned by most of those who once professed it. In its day, it had the beneficial effect of getting philosophers to look more closely at the logical status of different kinds of both meaningful and meaningless utterances. It is this that Ryle had in mind when he said, in the quotation given earlier, that the verification principle helped philosophers to see that there are different ways in which an utterance can be significant, or meaningful, and different ways in which it can be nonsensical. One important product of this insight into the diversity of meaning, as we shall see in Part 4, was Austin's theory of speech acts.

Truth-conditions

Like verificationism, one of its historical antecedents, the truth-conditional theory of meaning comes in several slightly different versions. What they have in common is their acceptance of the following thesis: to give an account of the meaning of a sentence is to specify the conditions under which it would be true or false of the situation, or state of the world, that it purports to describe. Alternatively, it is said that to know the meaning of a sentence is to know the conditions under which it (or the statement made by uttering it) would be true or false. Neither of these formulations is very precise as it stands, and they are not necessarily equivalent. For example, neither of them actually identifies the meaning of a sentence with its truth-conditions; and the second leaves open the question of what precisely is meant by knowing the truth-conditions of a sentence. We shall return to such questions in the following chapter.

For the present it suffices to draw the reader's attention to the difference between the *truth-value* of a proposition and the *truth-conditions* of a sentence. To take a simple example:

'John Smith is unmarried'

purports to express a set of propositions, each of which has a particular truth-value according to whether whoever (or whatever) is being referred to by 'John Smith', in actual utterances of this sentence, is unmarried or not. We do not need to know whether any particular John Smith is unmarried in order to know what *conditions* the world must satisfy for the proposition 'John Smith is unmarried' to be true. In cases like this at least, we know how we might verify (or falsify) empirically any one of the propositions that a sentence purports to express.

Also, independently of any empirical investigation relating to John Smith's marital status, we can argue, on the basis of our knowledge of English, as to whether

'John Smith is not married'

or even

'John Smith is a bachelor'

has the same truth-conditions as 'John Smith is unmarried'; and if they do, we can say that they have the same *propositional content*. A moment's reflection will tell us that 'John Smith is a bachelor' differs truth-conditionally from both of the others. Not every unmarried entity is a bachelor (for example, unmarried women are not, and there is nothing in the structure of English that prohibits us from referring to a woman as John Smith or, shall we say, George Eliot). The situation with respect to 'John Smith is unmarried' and 'John Smith is not married' is less clear-cut. But the principle is the same: *sentences have the same propositional content if and only if they have the same truth-conditions*. I leave it to the reader to put his understanding of the principle of truth-conditional equivalence to the test at this point by trying to falsify the statement that 'John Smith is unmarried' and 'John Smith is not married' have the same propositional content.

I have emphasized the historical connection between verificationism and truth-conditional semantics. Many authors would not have done this. But all the points made above about verificationism are relevant, in my view, to a proper understanding of truth-conditional semantics; and we shall draw upon them later. They could have been made in respect of truth-conditional semantics without mentioning logical positivism and verifiability. It is important to realize, however, that when it comes to the construction of a truth-conditional theory of meaning for natural languages, verifiability (or falsifiability) continues to present problems. It will not do to dismiss them on the grounds that verificationism itself has failed. As we have seen several times already, it is unreasonable to expect that competent speakers of a language should always be able to decide whether two expressions are necessarily true of the same classes of entities or not. If the truth-conditional theory of semantics is so construed that it rules out what seems to be a genuine indeterminacy in the semantic structure of natural languages, it may be rejected without more ado. But it need not be construed in this way. And it will not be so construed in what follows.

Tautologies and contradictions

Two kinds of propositions that are of particular concern to logicians and semanticists are *tautologies* and *contradictions*. The former, as traditionally defined, are propositions which are necessarily true by virtue of their *logical*

form. An example would be
"Either it is raining or it is not raining".
Contradictions, on the other hand, are propositions that are necessarily false by virtue of their logical form. For example:
"It is raining and it is not raining".
What is meant by 'logical form' in this context varies somewhat according to which system of logic we are operating with. But the above propositions would be shown to be tautologous and contradictory, respectively, in standard propositional logic by the definition of negation ("not"), conjunction ("both … and"), and disjunction ("either … or …").

It will be noted that I am using double quotation-marks at this point, because we are not concerned with English sentences as such, but rather with the propositions which they purport to express. (This use of double quotation-marks has been established in earlier chapters and is consistent with the general convention whereby expressions are distinguished notationally from their meanings.) It is important to emphasize once again that propositions, not sentences, are the bearers of truth and falsity.

Obviously, in construing "It is raining and it is not raining" as contradictory we have to make certain assumptions about the time and place being referred to: in particular, we must assume that we are not referring to different times and/or different places in the two constituent simpler propositions. "It is raining in Manchester and it is not raining in Timbuktu" is not contradictory. One might think that nothing but pedantry is involved in making points like this explicit. But, as we shall see later, there are important theoretical reasons for keeping such seemingly trivial points in mind.

Provided that we do keep this point in mind and draw the distinction between sentences and propositions when it needs to be drawn, we can extend the application of the terms 'tautology' and 'contradiction' to sentences in a

natural way. We can say of the sentences
    'Either it is raining or it is not (raining)'
and
    'It is raining and it is not (raining)'
that, taken at face-value, they are tautologous and contra-dictory, respectively. (By taking them at face-value, I mean interpreting them in terms of their purported propositional content and on the assumption that they are being used characteristically.) One of the principal tasks of semantic theory is to show how and why competent speakers of a language will recognize that some sentences are tautologous and others contradictory (unless there are good reasons in context for construing them otherwise than at their face-value).

Logical truths, or tautologies, are a subclass of *analytic* truths: that is, propositions whose truth is determined wholly by their meaning (cf. Chapter 4). However, lin-guists commonly extend the terms 'tautology' and 'contra-diction' to cover, not only those propositions (and sentences) whose truth or falsity is determined by logical form as this is traditionally conceived, but all kinds of analytically true or false propositions (and sentences). Thus, they would say that
    'This bachelor is unmarried'
is a tautologous sentence, and
    'This bachelor is married'
is a contradictory sentence, in that the first purports to express a tautology and the second a contradiction (on the assumption that 'bachelor' is taken in the relevant sense). We shall follow this practice.

Tautologies and, especially, contradictions are some-times classified as being semantically anomalous. Taken at face-value they are uninformative: they cannot be used to tell someone facts of which he was previously unaware or facts which he could not deduce himself on the basis of his knowledge of the language and the ability to draw valid inferences from what he already knows. And yet, whatever 'semantically anomalous' or 'meaningless' means in relation to tautologies and contradictions, it cannot mean "devoid of sense" (if 'sense' is construed technically in terms of propositional content). For tautologies and contradictions, as we have just seen, are by definition necessarily true and necessarily false respectively; and this implies that contradictory sentences, no less than tautologous sentences, must have determinable truth-conditions. The former are false and the latter true, as Leibniz put it, *in all possible worlds*. We can argue on both theoretical and empirical grounds about the range of data that is, or should be, covered by the terms 'tautology' and 'contradiction' (that is to say, about the coverage of the term 'analytic'). But we cannot without inconsistency abandon the principle that analytically true and false sentences are meaningful in the sense of having a propositional content.

Meaningless sentences

In conclusion, it is worthwhile looking again briefly at such sentences as

      'Colourless green ideas sleep furiously',

      'Quadruplicity drinks procrastination',

      'Thursday is in bed with Friday',

which we classified as grammatical, but meaningless, in the opening section of this chapter. There has been a good deal of discussion among liguists about the status of such sentences in recent years. Indeed, it has been argued that some or all of them are not even syntactically well-formed (and therefore are not English sentences at all). But this view has not prevailed. Apart from its implausibility in terms of the criteria of corrigibility and translatability mentioned earlier, it has the effect of making such sentences as

      'Colourless green ideas cannot possibly sleep furiously',

'It is obvious that quadruplicity does not drink procrastination',

'Thursday is said to have been in bed with Friday' difficult to account for either syntactically or semantically. The more interesting question is whether we were right to say that the sentences in question are meaningless.

According to the principle established in this section, 'Colourless green ideas sleep furiously', etc., cannot be devoid of sense – though they may be meaningless, or semantically anomalous, in other respects – if they are contradictory. But are they contradictory?

It is obvious that, since "X is green" entails "X is coloured" (by virtue of the sense-relation of hyponymy: cf. Chapter 4), 'Colourless green ideas sleep furiously' contains at least one contradictory expression. And no entity in any possible world could be both wholly without colour and even partly green, red, blue, etc. It also seems clear that only physical objects can be coloured and only animate beings can sleep. So on the assumption that ideas not only are not, but by virtue of the meaning of 'idea' could not be, physical objects – still less animate beings – 'Colourless green ideas sleep furiously' might be held to contain two further contradictions.

But is this assumption valid? There is little doubt that most rational speakers of English would say that it is. And yet rationality is notoriously unstable and culture-dependent with respect to what is held to be physical and non-physical, or animate and inanimate. In the last resort, it may be impossible to draw a sharp distinction between genuine contradictions (in the extended sense of the term) and propositions that are literally uninterpretable for us only because we are constrained, in our unsuccessful attempts to interpret them, by a particular set of assumptions about the nature of the world. Although the sentences we are discussing clearly violate the assumptions with which most of us operate, they seem to do so, intuitively at least, in different degrees and in different ways.

Many scholars have taken the view that all kinds of semantic anomaly – that is, everything that falls within the scope of the pre-theoretical notion of not making sense – can be brought together and accounted for theoretically in terms of a suitably extended concept of contradiction. An alternative, and arguably more traditional, view is that there is a distinction to be drawn between contradiction and what I will call *categorial incongruity*: between sentences that purport to express necessarily, or analytically, false propositions and sentences that have no propositional content at all. (We will return later to the notion of categorial incongruity. As we shall see, it is in connection with categorial incongruity that the problem of distinguishing grammatical from semantic unacceptability arises most acutely for the linguist.) Meanwhile, it may be observed that many linguists working within the framework of generative grammar have been inclined to take too restricted a view of semantic acceptability and have classified as literally uninterpretable (or necessarily false) a whole range of sentences that should not be so classified.

It was pointed out in the first section of this chapter that 'Colourless green ideas', etc., can be given various non-literal interpretations, provided that they are appropriately contextualized and the meaning of one or more of the constituent words is extended beyond its basic, or usual, sense. It is now apparent that many such sentences, which are literally uninterpretable in terms of our normal assumptions about the world in which we live, are readily interpretable, in their literal sense, if we are able and willing to relax or abandon these assumptions. For example,

> 'The stars will remember the night we said *Goodbye*',
> 'My lawnmower refused to start',
> 'The sergeant major barked out the order',
> 'Your friend's husband is a snake'

and indefinitely many such sentences, taken literally,

violate the ontological assumptions of most rational speakers of English, though to a much smaller degree than 'Colourless green ideas sleep furiously', etc. They can be literally interpreted without difficulty and should certainly not be classified as semantically anomalous. Nevertheless, the fact that they do violate our everyday assumptions about the world means that we will usually try to make sense of them, as we do with contradictions, by assigning to them something other than their purported literal sense. The principles whereby we make sense of sentences which, of themselves and construed literally, are contradictory or do not seem to make sense will occupy us briefly in Part 4.

Summary

In this chapter, I have explained something of the historical background to modern truth-conditional semantics. I have given particular emphasis to the fact that sentences as such cannot be classified as true or false independently of the contexts in which they are uttered. In this connection I have drawn a distinction between propositions and propositional content. We shall exploit this distinction to the full in all that follows.

Our discussion of the connection between meaning and truth has been sandwiched between two sections dealing with meaningful and meaningless sentences. This is a topic to which we shall return in Chapter 7. But first we must develop, in greater detail, our understanding of the relation between sentence-meaning and propositional content.

6 *Logical Links*

Sentence-meaning and propositional content

' "Contrariwise," continued Tweedledee, "if it was so, it might be; and if it were so, it would be; but as it isn't, it ain't. That's logic." '

Lewis Carroll, *Through the Looking Glass*

Grammatical theory and logic have been closely associated for centuries. Indeed, much of the terminology of traditional grammar – 'subject', 'predicate', 'mood', etc. – is also part of the logician's stock in trade. But does this use of the same terminology reflect anything more than a historical association between the two disciplines? Does the grammatical structure of a sentence correspond directly to the logical form of the proposition it expresses? Many people unthinkingly assume that this is so. It is not uncommon, for example, to hear someone asserting boldly that 'I haven't done nothing' must mean "I have done something" on the grounds that two negatives make a positive. Is this assumption valid? More generally, is there nothing more to the meaning of a sentence than its propositional content?

This chapter will show that there are certain aspects of sentence-meaning that cannot be adequately represented by standard propositional logic.

Parts of the chapter may seem somewhat technical to those not acquainted with modern formal logic. But none of the concepts that will be invoked is inherently difficult to understand. And it is only by looking at some of the points where propositional logic fails to give a full account of sentence-meaning that we can begin to appreciate both the achievements and the limitations of modern truth-conditional semantics – an approach to the analysis of sentence-meaning that is currently being followed by many outstanding scholars.

Thematic meaning

Sentences have the same propositional content if and only if they have the same truth-conditions. This is the principle that was established in the preceding chapter; and we shall stick to it throughout. We shall also continue to identify the propositional content of a sentence with its sense and, for present purposes, with its descriptive meaning. Our main concern in this chapter is to pose, and in part to answer, the following question: "How much of the meaning of a sentence is included within its propositional content?"

One part of the meaning of a sentence that is definitely not part of its propositional content is its *thematic meaning*. For example, the following sentences, which differ in thematic meaning, all have the same truth-conditions, and therefore the same propositional content:

'I have not read this book',
'This book I have not read',
'It is this book (that) I have not read',
'This book has not been read by me'.

So too do the following:

'A man is standing under the apple-tree',
'There is a man standing under the apple-tree'.

This kind of meaning is called thematic because it is very largely determined by the way a speaker presents what he is talking about (the *theme* of his utterance) in relation to particular contextual presuppositions. Frequently, but not always, what the speaker presents as thematic is also given elsewhere in the context and can be taken for granted as being known to the hearer or readily identifiable by him.

Actually, it is by no means clear that the two sets of sentences listed above are different sentences. It might be argued that the difference between, say, 'I have not read this book' and 'This book I have not read' has nothing to do with the grammatical or semantic structure of sentences, but rather with the utterance of the same sentence in one contextually determined word-order or another. Issues of this kind will occupy us in Part 4, when we look more closely at what is involved in the utterance of a sentence. For the moment, it may be observed that thematic meaning is primarily, if not wholly, a matter of utterance-meaning. Just how much, if any, is also to be regarded as a part of sentence-meaning is open to doubt.

It should also be noted that it is somewhat unrealistic to discuss thematic meaning without making reference to stress and intonation. Much the same communicative effect can be achieved by putting heavy stress on *this book* in the utterance of 'I have not read this book' as can be achieved by uttering 'This book I have not read'. Furthermore, when the latter sentence is uttered, it will not only have a non-neutral word-order, in contrast with the former sentence, but also a non-neutral intonation-contour. There is no general consensus among linguists as to how much of this thematically significant variation in the *prosodic* structure of utterances is to be accounted for in terms of sentence structure.

One point, however, is clear. It is part of one's linguistic competence to be able to control and interpret variations of word-order and grammatical structure of the kind that are exemplified in the sentences cited above. It is also part of one's linguistic competence to be able to control and interpret functionally comparable differences of stress and intonation. We cannot, therefore, hold simultaneously to the following two principles:

(i) Linguistic competence is restricted to the knowledge of sentence-structure;

(ii) All aspects of sentence-meaning are truth-conditional.

If we want to maintain (i), we must accept a much broader conception of sentence-structure than is traditional and, in doing so, abandon (ii). Alternatively, if we wish to defend (ii), we must either accept a much narrower conception of sentence-structure than is traditional or define thematic meaning to be something other than meaning.

Simple and composite sentences

A simple sentence, in traditional grammar, is a sentence that contains only one clause. What I am calling composite sentences – there is no generally accepted term for non-simple sentences – fall into two classes: compound and complex. The former may be analysed, at their highest level of structure, into two or more co-ordinate clauses; the latter into a main clause (which may be simple or composite) and at least one subordinate clause. Although these traditional distinctions are not without their problems, we can use them satisfactorily enough in our general discussion of the propositional content of sentences.

Roughly comparable with the distinction between simple and composite sentences is the distinction drawn in logic between simple and composite propositions. (What I am calling composite propositions are usually referred to as complex, and occasionally as compound. However, it seems preferable in the present context to standardize the grammatical and the logical terminology as far as possible.) But no distinction can be drawn among different kinds of composite propositions that matches, in any significant way, the grammatical distinction between compound and complex sentences. For example,

> 'If he passed his driving test, I am a Dutchman'

is complex, whereas

> 'Either he did not pass his driving test or I am a Dutchman'

is compound. The propositions expressed by the above two sentences are normally formalized in the propositional calculus by means of *implication* and *disjunction*, respectively: "*p* implies *q*", on the one hand, and "either not-*p* or *q*", on the other. At first sight, these two propositions look as if they might differ significantly in logical form, but they do not. They have exactly the same truth-value. Granted that "*p* implies *q*" and "either not-*p* or *q*" correctly formalize the range of propositions that can be asserted by uttering our sample complex and compound sentences, it follows that the sentences in question must have the same propositional content.

And yet one might hesitate to say that, as sentences, they have the same meaning. Even more striking are examples like:

> 'She was poor and she was honest',
> 'She was poor but she was honest',
> 'Although she was poor, she was honest'.

Most people would probably say that all three sentences differ in meaning, but that the second, which is compound, is closer in meaning to the third, a complex sentence, than it is to the first, which is another compound sentence. Once again, however, the composite propositions expressed by these sentences are equivalent. So, any difference of sentence-meaning that there might be among them is not a matter of propositional content.

The point is that the operations whereby composite propositions are formed out of simple propositions are, by definition, *truth-functional*. This means that the truth-value of a composite proposition is fully determined by – is a *function* of (in the specialized mathematical sense of 'function' explained in Chapter 4) – the truth-values of its constituent propositions and the specified effect of each operation. For example, *conjunction* (&) creates a composite proposition (p & q: "p and q") which is true if, and only if, both p and q are true. Similarly, *disjunction* (V), mentioned earlier, creates a composite proposition (p V q: "either p or q") which is true if, and only if, either p or q is true. And *negation* ($\sim$) creates a composite proposition ($\sim p$) out of a simple proposition (p); and $\sim p$ is defined to be true when p is false and false when p is true. It is doubtful, to say the least, whether the operations associated with the formation of composite sentences in natural languages are purely truth-functional.

Even the co-ordination of clauses by means of *and* is problematical from this point of view. This is the most neutral kind of conjunctive co-ordination in English. Its closest equivalent in the propositional calculus is undoubtedly conjunction (&). Very often, however, there is felt to be some kind of temporal or causal link between the situations described by the constituent propositions, such that the ordering of the clauses expressing these propositions is semantically significant. For example,

'John arrived late and missed the train'

and

'John missed the train and arrived late'

would normally be used in different circumstances. To make the point briefly, but crudely: *and* here appears to mean "and then" or "and therefore". Obviously, if *and* does have this meaning, it is not equivalent to the connective for propositional conjunction, &. For p & q has the same truth-values as q & p.

But does *and* – more precisely, the co-ordination of clauses in sequence by means of *and* – actually have the meaning "and then" or "and therefore"? An alternative view is that "then" or "therefore" is not part of the propositional content, but something that is merely implied (in a broad sense of 'imply') by our general tendency to adhere to the communicative norms of relevance and orderliness. Those who hold this view would argue that, in normal circumstances and in default of contextual information to the contrary, we can reasonably infer from the utterance of 'John arrived late and missed the train' that John's late arrival was the cause of his missing the train – even though there is nothing in the actual meaning of the sentence that gives us this information – because we can assume that the speaker is not misleading us by deliberately and gratuitously flouting the ground-rules. (It is not difficult to think of circumstances in which this sentence could be uttered to assert two otherwise unconnected facts. But, arguably, these circumstances must be clear from the context.) This argument has been used, and in the case of *and* persuasively, by the adherents of truth-conditional semantics. We shall come back to it in Chapter 9.

The arguments are rather less persuasive when they are used in support of the thesis that sentences containing *but* or *although* have the same meaning as sentences containing *and*, as in the sentences mentioned earlier: 'She was poor but she was honest' and 'Although she was poor, she was honest'. If we concede the truth-functionality of what I have called the most neutral kind of conjunctive co-ordination, involving the use of *and*, we must also allow that a speaker may superimpose upon his utterance of a grammatically and lexically neutral compound sentence like 'She was poor and she was honest' a prosodic contour (comprising stress and intonation) that indicates his own feelings about the propositions expressed and the connection between them. For example, it is possible for a speaker to utter 'She was poor and she was honest' in such a way that, in asserting the conjunction of two propositions, p & q, he simultaneously reveals his surprise that both p and q should be true. In such circumstances, the speaker might equally well utter 'She was poor but she was honest', with the appropriate prosodic contour. There would be no difference in the composite proposition that he asserts, and no readily identifiable difference in the degree or nature of the feelings that he reveals or indicates. Nevertheless, these two sentences differ in meaning, since *but*, unlike *and*, is never a purely neutral marker of propositional conjunction.

Similar problems arise, in certain languages, in connection

with disjunction. For example, in Latin there are two ways of translating English *either-or* sentences. One can use the particles ... *vel* ... *vel* ... or alternatively the particles ... *aut* ... *aut* .... It has been suggested, at times, that the difference between them is that the *vel*-construction is used for inclusive disjunction and the *aut*-construction for exclusive disjunction. An inclusive disjunction, $p \lor q$, is true, not only if either p or q is true and the other false, but also if both p and q are true. An exclusive disjunction, on the other hand, is true only if either p is true and q false or q is true and p false: it excludes the possibility of both p and q being true. Usually, when logicians use the term 'disjunction' without qualification they mean "inclusive disjunction". To return, then, to the Latin example. In fact, it does not seem to be the case, except perhaps in the specialized usage of logicians, that *vel* is used for inclusive and *aut* for exclusive disjunction. What is true, however, is that the *aut*-construction is stronger or more expressive than the *vel*-construction in much the same way that *but* conjunction is stronger and more expressive than *and* conjunction in English. It is difficult to be more precise than this without attributing to *aut*, in contrast with *vel*, several distinct meanings. Perhaps the best way of explaining what is meant by 'stronger and more expressive' in this context is to say that the nearest equivalent to the *aut*-construction in English is (*either*) ... *or* ... with heavy stress on the disjunctive particles. Much the same effect is achieved in French by adding *bien* to the otherwise neutral disjunctive particles (*ou*) ... *ou* ..., and in Russian by adding *že*. In some contexts, stronger or more expressive disjunction will indeed be understood to be exclusive; in others, however, it will indicate that, in the speaker's opinion, the alternatives p and q are the only propositions worth considering and will dramatize, or emphasize, the necessity of opting for one or the other. The distinction between inclusive and exclusive disjunction can be accounted for truth-functionally; the distinction between neutral and stronger, or more expressive, disjunction cannot.

Mention should be made, finally, of the so-called paradoxes of implication: $p \rightarrow q$ ("p implies q"). These may look rather forbidding when they are set out in full detail and with ample use of symbolism in textbooks of logic, but the point at issue is very important and not difficult to understand. Implication is usually rendered into English by means of a conditional sentence: for example, 'If he passed his driving test, his parents have bought him a Porsche'. But "p implies q" is true, by definition, not only when both p and q are true, but also whenever p is false. So the proposition expressed by 'If he passed his driving test, his parents have bought him a Porsche' (if it has the logical form of "p implies q") is true even if the person referred to by 'he' did not pass the driving test, provided only that his parents have bought him a Porsche. Most people find this paradoxical. Furthermore, the truth-value of "p implies q", like that of "p and q", is totally independent of any causal connection between the situations described by each of the constituent propositions. For example, the proposition expressed by 'If Lady Godiva had blue eyes, his parents have bought him a Porsche' would be true (independently of the colour of Lady Godiva's eyes) if the parents of the person referred to by 'he', on some occasion of the utterance of the sentence, have indeed bought him a Porsche. Once again, most people find this paradoxical – unless, of course, they can discern some kind of connection, in context, between the propositional content of the two clauses. It is always possible to devise a plausible connection for any two clauses in any conditional sentence and thereby eliminate the apparent paradox; and the full importance of this fact will emerge in our treatment of the notion of relevance in Chapter 9. But what if we do not seek to eliminate the so-called paradoxes of implication in this way?

The conditional sentence given earlier, 'If he passed his

driving test, I am a Dutchman', is interesting (but highly untypical) from this point of view; and this is why I chose it! As it would normally be used (by non-Dutchmen), it depends for its effect upon the known falsity of q ("I am a Dutchman") and the presumed absence of any causal link between the situations described by p ("He passed his driving test") and q. Under these circumstances, we might well be prepared to say that the composite proposition expressed by the sentence as a whole is equivalent to the one expressed by 'Either he did not pass his driving test or I am a Dutchman', and that it is true if both p and q are false. But this is surely because the utterance of this sentence is rhetorically equivalent to the denial of p in a context in which the assertion of q is non-informative. In other words, the speaker can trade on the hearer's knowledge that the speaker is not a Dutchman and the hearer's consequential ability to infer the falsity of p ("He passed his driving test") from the truth of the presumably informative composite proposition "p implies q". The speaker can be all the more certain that the hearer will draw the correct inference in a case like this because the proposition "I am a Dutchman" has been conventionalized in English-speaking circles for this very purpose. However, any sufficiently preposterous or self-evidently false proposition will serve the same rhetorical purpose ("If he has got a degree in linguistics, I am the Queen of Sheba", etc.). We do indeed make rhetorical, or as many would say these days pragmatic, use of at least a subclass of conditional sentences in the way that I have just illustrated.

To summarize, then: the formation of many kinds of composite sentences in English and other natural languages does not seem to be purely truth-functional. In some cases there is the addition of a non-propositional, expressive, element (cf. *but* conjunction and the Latin *aut*-construction); in others, there is doubt as to the validity of truth-functional considerations at all (cf. the so-called paradoxes of implication). It would seem, therefore, that the meaning of composite sentences is not always exhausted by their propositional content – even when this is determinable.

Negation

As we have just seen, negation (symbolized by '$\sim$') is regarded by logicians as an operation which forms a composite proposition ($\sim p$) out of a simple proposition (p). As far as standard, two-valued, propositional logic is concerned, the truth-functional definition of negation is straightforward: when p is true, $\sim p$ is false; and when p is false, $\sim p$ is true. It is further allowed that negation should be recursive, so that the negation of $\sim p$ yields $\sim\sim p$, which is equivalent to p (two negatives make a positive), the negation of $\sim\sim p$ yields $\sim\sim\sim p$, which is equivalent to $\sim p$, and so on. How does the standard logical account of negation relate to the meaning and use of negative sentences in natural languages? More particularly, how much of the meaning of negative constructions is part of the propositional content of sentences?

There are various ways in which negative sentences are constructed in natural languages. Only rarely, however, is there any reason to say that a negative sentence is grammatically composite by contrast with the corresponding positive, or affirmative, sentence. Generally speaking, corresponding sentences of opposite *polarity* have the same clause-structure, and what we can identify most easily with propositional negation applies within clauses and does not extend to whole sentences. Indeed, in many languages the negative polarity of a clause (like its mood or its tense) is marked not by means of a separate word-form like the English *not*, but by special forms of the verb, or predicate. Hence, the traditional maxim: negation of the predicate is equivalent to negation of the proposition.

But there is one kind of predicate-negation which is

clearly not equivalent to negation of the whole proposition. This may be exemplified by

'John is unfriendly',

which, unlike

'John is not friendly',

expresses a proposition that is not just the contradictory of the proposition expressed by

'John is friendly',

but its contrary. In other words, "John is unfriendly" is not simply the negation of "John is friendly": it implies "John is hostile". It is quite possible for John to be neither friendly nor unfriendly. (Of course, 'John is not friendly' is often used in everyday conversation as if it had the same sense as 'John is unfriendly'. More important, there is also a way of uttering 'John is not friendly' which makes it clear that the negation applies only to the predicative expression 'friendly'. But this does not concern us here.)

There are three ways of handling this fact. The first, which is excluded by the formulation I have just used, is to say that there are two distinct sentences represented in written English by 'John is not friendly' and that they are distinguished, at least optionally, in spoken English by means of rhythm and intonation. But rhythm and the fine differences of intonation that are involved in cases like this are universally excluded by linguists from what they consider to be part of the prosodic structure of sentences. The second way is to say that there is one sentence, but that it is structurally ambiguous. The third is to draw upon the distinction between sentence-meaning and utterance-meaning and to say that 'John is not friendly' is a single unambiguous sentence which can be uttered in a particular way, and perhaps also in identifiable contexts, with more or less the same communicative effect as the utterance of 'John is unfriendly'. Let us simply opt, without argument, for the third of the three possible analyses.

It is also possible to have negated nominal expressions

occurring as clause-constituents. For example,

'Non-students pay the full entrance fee'

expresses a proposition which differs from, and does not
entail, the proposition expressed by

'Students do not pay the full entrance fee.'

Nominal negation of this kind ('non-students'), like predicative negation ('do not pay'), has an effect on the
propositional content of the clause in which it occurs and
is in principle truth-functional; but it cannot be formalized
in standard propositional logic.

To be contrasted with nominal negation of the kind
exemplified by 'non-students' above is the use of negative
indefinite pronouns like 'no one' or 'nothing' or the
semantically comparable nominals introduced with the
adjectival 'no' (e.g., 'no man': cf. French 'aucun homme',
German 'kein Mensch', etc.). It is obvious, upon reflection if not immediately, that

'No one telephoned'

expresses a proposition which contradicts the proposition
expressed by

'Someone telephoned',

whereas

'Someone did not telephone',

which looks as if it is the negative sentence that most
directly corresponds to 'someone telephoned', can be
conjoined with 'someone did not telephone' to express
the non-contradictory composite proposition,

"Someone telephoned and someone did not telephone".

Most logicians and linguists have taken the view, until
recently at least, that the proposition expressed by 'No
one telephoned' differs in logical form from the proposition expressed by, say,

'John telephoned'.

The most notable difference between 'No one telephoned'
and 'John telephoned', from this point of view, is that the
latter (when it is used to make a statement) is associated
with a particular kind of *existential presupposition*: that is,

it conveys the speaker's presupposition that there exists some entity that may be appropriately referred to with the expression 'John'. There is no such existential presupposition associated with the use of 'nobody', 'nothing', etc.

Consideration of sentences like those listed above within a more comprehensive discussion of negation in English and other languages raises further problems. How are positive sentences containing 'some' related grammatically and semantically to corresponding negative sentences containing 'any'? (What is the relation, for example, between 'He saw someone' and 'He did not see anyone'?) And how are they related to corresponding negative sentences containing 'some'? (Does 'He saw no one' mean exactly the same as 'He did not see anyone'?) Problems like this, involving the complex interaction of negation, the use of determiners, quantifiers and indefinite pronouns (and adjectives), etc., have been extensively treated by linguists in recent years. In some cases, the facts themselves are in dispute, especially when it comes to alleged differences of meaning which cannot be accounted for truth-functionally. But it is very difficult to handle even the undisputed cases of propositional negation, in a theoretically unified framework within which grammatical structure and logical form can be put into correspondence simply and systematically.

Negation is an operation that applies to a single expression. But the expression in question can be simple or composite. In $\sim p$ the expression to which the operator applies – the expression that is in its *scope* – is simple, whereas in $\sim(p \ \& \ q)$ it is composite. Everything within the matching left and right parentheses that immediately follow the negation-operator is in its scope; in default of such parentheses the negation-operator is taken to apply to the smallest expression on its right. There is therefore a significant difference between $\sim(p \ \& \ q)$ and $\sim p \ \& \ q$: between, say, "Mary was not well-and-cheerful" and "Mary was not-well and cheerful" (if I may informally indicate the difference by means of hyphens).

It is easy to see that there are other such differences of scope in respect of propositional negation in natural languages. For example,

'John did not kiss Mary because she was his sister' can be construed in two ways: (i) "It was because she was his sister that John did not kiss Mary", and (ii) "It was not because she was his sister that John kissed Mary". Under interpretation (i), the sentence in question is taken to be one in which negation applies only to the propositional content of the main clause ("John kissed Mary"); under interpretation (ii), it is a sentence in which negation applies to the content of the subordinate clause ("because she was his sister") or, arguably, to the composite proposition "John kissed Mary because she was his sister". Of course, the difference between (i) and (ii) is not correctly formalized in terms of the truth-functional difference between $\sim p$ & q and $\sim(p$ & $q)$. As we have seen, the propositional calculus cannot draw the distinction between conjunction and causal subordination. Nevertheless, it is intuitively clear that the difference between (i) and (ii) is, in principle, formalizable in terms of the scope of propositional negation. There are many such examples.

The scope of negation is also relevant in modal logic, which extends the propositional calculus by means of the logical operators of necessity (N) and possibility (M). "It is not necessary that p" ($\sim Np$) differs truth-functionally from "It is necessary that not-p" ($N\sim p$). For example, "The sky is not necessarily blue" differs in truth-value from "Necessarily, the sky is not blue". As we shall see in Part 4, at least some of what can be identified as modality in natural languages can be ascribed to the propositional content of sentences. In such cases, there is often a fairly straightforward correspondence between the scope of negation and grammatical structure. For example,

'He may not come' can be construed, syntactically, in two ways, according to whether *not* has narrower or wider scope than the modal verb 'may': (i) "It is possible that he will not come"

($M{\sim}p$), in contrast with (ii) "It is not possible/allowed that he will come" (${\sim}Mp$).

What cannot be formalized, even in modal logic, is the difference between the assertion of a negative proposition ("I say that it is not raining") and the denial of a positive proposition ("I deny that it is raining"); or again, the difference between the assertion of a positive proposition ("I say that it is raining") and the denial of a negative proposition ("I deny that it is not raining"). Here, too, we have differences that can be accounted for in terms of the scope of negation. Moreover, they are differences that are reflected, at least partly, in the syntactic and prosodic structure of sentences. But assertion and denial are not, and cannot be, constituents of propositions or propositional content; they are different kinds of communicative acts. Insofar as the difference between assertion and denial, and between other kinds of communicative acts, is systematically encoded in what was earlier referred to as the face-value of sentences, it is yet another part of the meaning of sentences that is not part of their propositional content.

Sentence-type and mood

It is by now common enough for linguists to draw a terminological distinction between declarative sentences and statements, between interrogative sentences and questions, between imperative sentences and commands, between exclamative sentences and exclamations. It is far less common for them to point out that, in traditional usage, there is a crucial difference between 'declarative', 'interrogative' and 'exclamative', on the one hand, and 'imperative', on the other. The former set of terms subclassify sentences according to what I will call *sentence-type*. The term 'imperative', however, goes rather with 'indicative', 'subjunctive', 'optative', 'conditional', etc., and subclassifies not sentences, but clauses; and it subclassifies them according to *mood*.

There is a connection between sentence-type and mood. But they are partly independent dimensions of the grammatical structure of sentences, and it is important not to confuse them. In particular, it is important not to confuse 'declarative' with 'indicative', as philosophers and even linguists do at times. A sentence cannot be simultaneously interrogative and declarative; but it can be both interrogative and indicative – i.e., it can be interrogative in sentence-type and contain, as its sole or principal clause, one that is indicative in mood. But it can also be, in some languages if not in English, both interrogative and subjunctive. Similarly, a sentence can be declarative without being indicative. Indeed, there are languages in which there are various kinds of non-indicative declarative sentences, but no indicative sentences at all.

This point is of more than purely terminological interest. As we shall see in Part 4, it supports a tripartite analysis of the logical structure of both sentences and utterances in preference to the bipartite analysis favoured by many logicians and formal semanticists. For the present, however, we can let the term 'declarative sentence' stand for 'indicative declarative sentence'. This is how it is usually interpreted in recent work in semantics.

It is generally recognized that sentences other than declaratives present problems for truth-conditional theories of sentence-meaning. In many cases they can be put into correspondence with particular declaratives on the basis of their grammatical and lexical structure. For example, the interrogative sentence

    'Is the door open?'

is systematically related, it terms of its grammatical and lexical structure, to the declarative sentence

    'The door is open'.

And the systematic grammatical and lexical relation between the two would seem to reflect a no less systematic semantic relation. But what is the nature of this semantic relation? Intuitively, it would seem that they share much, if not all, of their propositional content, but differ with respect to the totality of their sentence-meaning.

There are several ways of assigning truth-conditions to 'Is the door open?', such that the similarity and difference between its meaning and that of 'The door is open' are systematically accounted for. One is to say that it has the same propositional content as

'I ask whether the door is open'.

But this is readily shown to be unsatisfactory, since the meaning of 'Is the door open?' is independent of its being used to ask a question. For example, there is nothing illogical or contradictory about the utterance

Is the door open? – that is a question which I refuse to ask.

And yet there should be if

'Is the door open?'

and

'I ask whether the door is open'

have the same meaning.

Another way of accounting fully for the sentence-meaning of 'Is the door open?' within the framework of truth-conditional semantics is by identifying it, semantically, with the set of declaratives, including 'The door is open', that may be used correctly or acceptably to answer it when it is uttered to ask a question. This approach to the semantic analysis of interrogatives has been adopted, and developed with great subtlety, in much recent work in formal semantics. It has its advantages from a purely logical point of view. But it is hardly the approach that would be chosen by someone who was not determined, for metatheoretical reasons, to force the whole of sentence-meaning into a truth-conditional straitjacket.

Much more attractive to anyone who favours the ancient scientific principle of saving the appearances is the view taken by Gottlob Frege, the German scholar whose seminal work on the philosophy of language in the late nineteenth century has been of central importance in the formalization of semantics. According to Frege, and his present-day followers, the meaning of 'Is the door open?' is composed of both a propositional and a non-propositional component. The propositional component, "The door is open", it shares with 'The door is open'; the non-propositional component is that part of its meaning by virtue of which it is used, characteristically, for questions rather than statements. But 'The door is open' also has a non-propositional component, namely that part of its meaning which makes it appropriate for uttering statements. Frege's formulation was slightly different from the one that I have just given, partly because he did not distinguish between sentences and utterances – or indeed, at times, between sentences, clauses and propositions ('Satz' in German covers all three). But my formulation preserves the substance of Frege's and adjusts it, terminologically and conceptually, to the broader notion of meaning adopted in this book.

I said that Frege's view, which does not require us to assign truth-conditions to non-declaratives, saves the appearances. The appearances, across a large sample of the world's languages, would certainly suggest that the meaning of corresponding declaratives and interrogatives of the kind exemplified by 'The door is open' and 'Is the door open?' respectively can be factorized into two parts. Generally speaking, in languages in which there is a clearly identifiable distinction between declaratives and interrogatives, the latter differ from the former in one of three ways: by a difference of word-order, by the occurrence of a special interrogative particle, or by morphological variation in the verb. It is sometimes said that there is another way of distinguishing declaratives and interrogatives: by means of intonation. Arguably, however, this kind of intonational difference, which in many languages distinguishes questions from statements, should be attributed, not to sentence-structure as such, but to the process and products of utterance. This is the view taken here. It means that there are languages (cf. Italian, Spanish, Modern Greek – to name but a few of the more familiar European languages) in which there is no difference, at the sentence-level, between declaratives and interrogatives of the kind, exemplified by 'The door is open' and 'Is the door open?'

Sentences that are grammatically neutral with respect to the distinction between declaratives and interrogatives (but can be used appropriately in the utterance of either statements or questions) are the only sentences whose meaning is exhausted by their propositional content. Sentences whose grammatical structure marks them as either declarative or interrogative have as the non-propositional component of their meaning their potential for use, characteristically, with one communicative function rather than another. And it is noteworthy that the grammatical structure of such sentences is often readily analysable into a propositional and a non-propositional part. Several versions of transformational grammer, including the earliest version developed by Chomsky (1957) and subsequently adopted (with modifications) by Katz and Postal (1964), have exploited this fact.

Exclamative and imperative sentences are different from declaratives and interrogatives, and from one another, in several respects. But the same general point can be made: in addition to their propositional content, they also encode and grammaticalize (in those languages in which the relevant distinctions are indeed grammaticalized) some kind of non-propositional meaning. As far as exclamative sentences are concerned, this non-propositional component of sentence-meaning is obviously expressive. What the non-propositional component in the meaning of imperative sentences is will be discussed later. So too will the non-propositional component of interrogative sentences. For the moment, it is sufficient to say that, as declarative sentences grammaticalize their characteristic use for making statements, so interrogative and imperative sentences grammaticalize their characteristic use for asking (or posing) questions and issuing commands, requests, entreaties, etc.

In English and many other languages, there is a structural similarity between exclamative sentences and dependent interrogative clauses. For example,

'How tall he is'

has the same structure, at least superficially, as the subordinate clause in

'I wonder how tall he is'.

Functionally, however, there is a clear difference between exclamatives of the kind exemplified by 'How tall he is' and interrogatives. In fact, exclamatives of this kind are best seen, semantically, as a subclass of expressive statements, in which the non-propositional part of what distinguishes the meaning of 'How tall he is' from the meaning of

'He is very tall'

is grammaticalized, rather than being expressed, in utterance, by a particular prosodic contour. It is because it is grammaticalized and is correlated with systematic restrictions on polarity, the use of modal verbs, etc., that 'How tall he is' is rightly regarded by grammarians as an exemplar of a distinct sentence-type. It is, of course, important not to confuse exclamatives with exclamations. Sentences of all types may be uttered with that particular expressive modulation which is conveyed in the spoken language by stress and intonation, and in the written language by means of the exclamation-mark. Exclamation is something very different from making statements, issuing commands and requests, and asking (or posing) questions.

Imperative sentences cannot be put into correspondence with declarative sentences as readily as interrogative sentences of the kind exemplified by 'Is the door open?' can. The reason is that mood is not independent of tense. Whereas 'Is the door open?' can be said to have the same propositional content as 'The door is open', it is not

obvious that
      'Open the door'
has the same propositional content as the declarative
sentence
      'You open the door',
if (a) tense is held to be a part of the propositional content
of a sentence and (b) the tense of 'You open the door' is
given its most usual interpretation. As far as condition (b)
is concerned, it should be noted that 'open' belongs to a
class of verbs – the majority in English – which do not
normally occur in the simple present with present-time
reference. Furthermore, from a semantic point of view it
might be argued that the time-reference of a request or
command made by uttering 'Open the door' is inherent in
the act of requesting or commanding, so that the sentence
itself is tenseless. Anyway, there is no doubt that mood
and tense are interdependent in all languages that have
both. And mood, whose function is usually if not always
non-propositional, is far more common throughout the
languages of the world than tense. Only a minority of
languages have tense; and many of the functions of tense
in those languages that have it are quite definitely non-
propositional. I will come back to this point in Part 4.
   Condition (a) is more important, and more controversial. All that needs to be said here is that from one point
of view – the point of view of classical logic –
propositions are eternally true or false, and therefore of
their very nature tenseless. It is when propositions are
treated as objects of mental acts or attitudes, on the one
hand, or of such communicative acts as assertion and
denial, on the other, that one is tempted to introduce
tense into propositions themselves, anchoring them to the
moment at which the mental or communicative act is
performed. We shall not be able to deal with the problem
of reconciling these two different views of propositions in
the present book. It should be noted, however, that it is a
problem that is all too often ignored in general treatments
of tense, not only by linguists, but also by logicians.

In fact, standard tense-logic, so called, is grossly inadequate for the analysis of tense as it actually operates in those natural languages that have it. But this fact is now coming to be appreciated. Richer and more powerful systems of tense-logic are being developed; and there is little doubt that our understanding of tense will be greatly advanced in the next few years.

What has just been said about tense holds true of many natural-language phenomena. It is not difficult to demonstrate the inadequacy of current treatments of natural languages within the framework of standard propositional logic. Much of this chapter has been devoted to just that task. But my purpose throughout has been constructive. We learn more from a demonstrably inadequate, but precisely formulated, theory than we do from one that is so vaguely expressed that we do not even see its inadequacy. Let us bear this point in mind as we move on to consider some of the recent work in formal semantics.

Summary

In this chapter, we have seen that there are several aspects of sentence-meaning that cannot be satisfactorily formalized within the framework of standard propositional logic: thematic meaning; the contribution that subordinating and co-ordinating conjunctions, or connectives, make to the meaning of complex and compound sentences; various kinds of negation; the meaning of sentences that are non-declarative in type and non-indicative in mood. At the same time, we have found no reason to deny that a major part of the descriptive meaning of sentences – their propositional content – is amenable to analysis with the tools and concepts of modern logic.

7 *Man-made Models*

The formalization of
sentence-meaning

'The world is the totality of facts, not of things.'
Ludwig Wittgenstein, *Tractatus*

This chapter follows on from the preceding one and looks
at two influential theories of sentence-meaning from the
viewpoint of formal semantics.

The first is the Katz-Fodor theory of meaning, which
originated in association with Chomsky's theory of transformational-generative grammar. The second is a particular version of possible-worlds semantics, initiated in the
late 1960s by Richard Montague, and widely recognized
as one of the most promising approaches to the truly
formidable task of accounting for the propositional content of sentences in a mathematically precise and elegant
manner.

The treatment of both theories is very selective and
almost completely non-technical. I have been more concerned to explain some of the basic concepts than to
introduce any of the formalism.

Formal semantics

The term 'formal semantics' can be given several different
interpretations. Originally, it meant "the semantic analysis of formal systems" – a formal system, or formal
language, being one that has been deliberately constructed by logicians, computer scientists, etc. for philosophical or practical purposes. More recently, the term
has been applied to the analysis of meaning in natural

languages, but usually with a number of restrictions, tacit or explicit, which derive from its philosophical and logical origins.

In particular, it is customarily associated with a restricted view of sentence-meaning; the view that sentence-meaning is exhausted by propositional content. As we have seen in Chapter 6, there are various kinds of meaning, which are plausibly attributed to sentences, but which are not readily accounted for in terms of their propositional content. Two reactions are open to the formal semanticist in the face of such difficulties. One is to say that what I have identified as a part of sentence-meaning is the product of something else; contextual assumptions and expectations, non-linguistic knowledge, conversational implicatures, etc. The second reaction is to accept that it is part of sentence-meaning and to attempt to provide a truth-conditional account of the phenomena – as some logicians have done, so far without much success, in respect of tense, mood and sentence-type.

It should be emphasized that the failure of formal semantics, so far, to account satisfactorily for such phenomena as tense, mood and sentence-type does not deprive the attempts that have been made to deal with them of all theoretical interest. The failure of a precise, but inadequate, account often points the way to the construction of an equally precise, but more comprehensive, theory of the same phenomena. And even when it does not do this, it may throw some light, obliquely and by reflection, upon the data that it does not fully illuminate. Many examples of this can be cited. To take but one: so far, no fully satisfactory account of the meaning of 'some' and 'any' (and their congeners: 'someone', 'anyone'; 'something', 'anything'; etc.) had been provided within the framework of formal semantics. Nevertheless, our understanding of the range of potentially relevant factors which determine the selection of one or the other has been greatly increased by the numerous attempts that have been made to handle the data truth-conditionally. Anyone who doubts this is invited to compare the treatment of 'any' and 'some' in older and more recent pedagogical grammars of English, not to mention scholarly articles on the topic. He will see the difference immediately.

What follows is a deliberately simplified account of some of the principal concepts of formal semantics that are of proven relevance to the analysis of the propositional content of sentences. Limitations of space oblige me to be selective and, at times, more allusive or dogmatic than I should like to be. The allusions are for the benefit of those who already have some background in linguistics. The dogmatism will be apparent to those who do not share my views. I take no account of anything other than what is uncontroversially a part of the propositional content of sentences in English.

Compositionality

The principle of *compositionality* has been mentioned already in connection with the sense of words and phrases. Commonly described as *Frege's principle*, it is more frequently discussed with reference to sentence-meaning. This is why I have left a fuller treatment of it for this chapter. It is central to formal semantics in all its developments. As it is usually formulated, it runs as follows (with 'composite' substituted for 'complex' or 'compound'): the meaning of a composite expression is a function of the meanings of its component expressions. Three of the terms used here deserve attention: 'meaning', 'expression' and 'function'. I will comment upon each of them in turn and then say why the principle of compositionality is so important.

'Meaning', as we have seen, can be given various interpretations. If we restrict it to descriptive meaning, or propositional content, we can still draw a distinction between sense and denotation (see Chapter 3). Frege's own distinction between sense and reference (drawn originally in German by means of the terms 'Sinn' and 'Bedeutung') is roughly comparable, and is accepted in broad outline, if not in detail, by most formal semanticists. I will take the principle of compositionality to apply primarily to sense.

The term 'expression' is usually left undefined when it is used by linguists. But it is normally taken to include sentences and any of their syntactically identifiable constituents. I have given reasons earlier for distinguishing expressions from forms, as far as words and phrases are concerned. For simplicity of exposition, I will now include sentences among the expressions of a language. More important, I will assume that there is an identifiable subpart of every sentence that is the bearer of its propositional content, and that this also is an expression to which the principle of compositionality applies.

The term 'function' is being employed in its mathematical sense: i.e., to refer to a rule, formula or operation which assigns a single *value* to each member of the set of entities in its *domain*. (It thus establishes either a many-one or one-to-one correspondence between the members of the domain, D, and the set of values, V: it *maps D* either into or on to V.) For example, there is an arithmetical function, normally written $y = x^2$, which for any numerical value of x yields a single and determinate numerical value for x^2. Similarly, in the propositional calculus there is a function which for each value of the propositional variables in every well-formed expression maps that expression into the two-member domain {True, False}. As we saw earlier, this is what is meant by saying that composite propositions are truth-functional. I have now spelled this out in more detail and deliberately introduced, with some redundancy, several of the technical terms that are commonly employed in formal semantics. We are advancing, in measured steps, to the point where we shall no longer blench when we are told that the sense, or intension, of an expression is a function from possible worlds to extensions. We shall not go into the technical details of formal semantics, but the limited amount of terminology introduced here will be useful to us later, and it will give readers with a knowledge of elementary set-theory some indication of the mathematical framework within which formal semantics operates.

But what is the relevance of all this to the semantic analysis of natural-language expressions? First of all, it should be noted that competent users of a language are able to interpret indefinitely many composite expressions of that language. Since it is impossible for anyone to have learned the sense of every composite expression in the way that he, presumably, learns the sense of lexemes, there must be some function which determines the sense of composite expressions on the basis of the sense of lexemes. Second, it is reasonable to assume that the sense of a composite expression is a function, not only of the sense of its component lexemes, but also of its grammatical structure. We have made this assumption throughout; and it can be tested empirically in a sufficient number of instances for us to accept it as valid. What we want then, in the ideal, is a precisely formulated procedure for the syntactic composition of all the well-formed lexically composite expressions in a language, coupled with a procedure for determining the semantic effect, if any, of each process or stage of syntactic composition. This is what formal semantics seeks to provide.

Formal semantics, as such, is not committed to any particular theory of syntax. Nor does it say anything in advance about the closeness of the correspondence between syntactic and semantic structure in natural languages. There is a wide range of options on each of these issues. I will consider only two of the best known approaches to the problem of determining that compositional function (whatever it is) which assigns sense to the lexically composite expressions of natural languages.

I will do so at a very general level, and I will restrict my treatment to what is uncontroversially a matter of propositional content. The two approaches are those of Chomskyan transformational grammar, on the one hand, and Montague grammar, on the other.

The Katz-Fodor theory

What I will refer to as the Katz-Fodor theory of sentence-meaning is not generally regarded as a theory of formal semantics, but I will treat it as such. It originated with a paper by J.J. Katz and J.A. Fodor, 'The structure of a semantic theory', first published in 1963. The theory itself has since been modified in various ways, notably by Katz, and has given rise to a number of alternatives, which I will not deal with here. Indeed, I will not even attempt to give a full account of the Katz-Fodor theory in any of its versions. I will concentrate upon two things: *projection rules* and *selection restrictions*.

The Katz-Fodor theory is formalized within the framework of Chomskyan generative grammar. It was the first such theory of semantics to be proposed, and it played an important part in the development of the so-called *standard theory* of transformational grammar, which Chomsky outlined in *Aspects of the Theory of Syntax* (1965). Looked at from a more general point of view, the Katz-Fodor theory can be seen as the first linguistically sophisticated attempt to give effect to the principle of compositionality. Traditional grammarians had for centuries emphasized the interdependence of syntax and semantics. Many of them had pointed out that the meaning of a sentence was determined partly by the meaning of the words it contained and partly by its syntactic structure. But they had not sought to make this point precise in relation to a generative theory of syntax – for the simple reason that generative grammar itself is of very recent origin.

For simplicity, I will discuss the Katz-Fodor theory in what may now be thought of as its classical version; not in its original formulation, but as it was presented in the period immediately following upon the publication of Chomsky's *Aspects*. The main consequence, as far as the general purpose of this book is concerned, is that I shall be taking for granted a particular notion of *deep structure* which has now been abandoned by almost all linguists, including Chomsky. The arguments for and against the classical notion of deep structure are interesting and important. But I shall not go into them here. Nor will I burden the text with unnecessary technical detail. The advantage of operating with the classical notion of deep structure, in a book of this kind, is that it is more familiar to non-specialists than any of the alternatives. And what I have to say about projection rules and selection restrictions is not materially affected by the adoption of one view of deep structure rather than another, or indeed by the abandonment of the notion of deep structure altogether.

According to the standard theory of transformational grammar, every sentence has two distinct levels of syntactic structure, linked by rules of a particular kind called transformations. These two levels are deep structure and surface structure. They differ formally in that they are generated by rules of a different kind. For our purposes the crucial point is that deep structure is more intimately connected with sentence-meaning than surface structure is. Surface structure, on the other hand, is more intimately connected with the way the sentence is pronounced. (As we shall see in Chapter 9, the process of uttering sentences, whether spoken or written, is more complex than this deliberately non-technical formulation of the relation between surface structure and pronunciation might suggest.) Omitting all but the bare essentials, we can represent the relation between syntax, semantics and phonology, diagrammatically, as in Figure 3 (cf. Lyons, 1977a:79).

With reference to this diagram, we can see that the grammar (in the broadest sense of the term) comprises

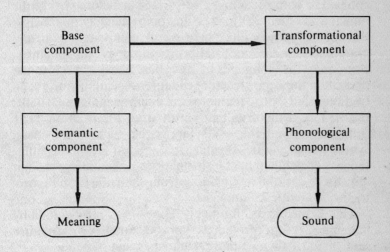

Fig. 3: The standard theory of transformational grammar. The deep structure of a sentence is the output of the base component and the input to both the transformational component and the semantic component; the surface structure of a sentence is the output of the transformational component and the input to the phonological component.

four sets of rules, which, operating as an integrated system, relate sound and meaning. The base component, it should be noted, contains, not only the non-transformational rules of syntax, for the language in question, but also its *lexicon*, or dictionary. And the lexicon provides for each lexeme in the language all the syntactic, semantic and phonological information that is necessary to distinguish that lexeme from others and to account for its occurrence in well-formed sentences. The base component, then, generates a set of deep structures, and the transformational component converts each of these into one or more surface structures.

I said earlier that deep structure is more intimately connected with meaning, and surface structure with pronunciation. Figure 3 makes this point clear by means of the arrows which link the several components of the grammar. All the information required by the semantic component is supplied by the base, and therefore is present in the deep structure of sentences; all the information required by the phonological component is present in the surface structures that result from the operation of transformational rules. As far as the relation between syntax and semantics is concerned, Figure 3 expresses the famous principle that transformations do not affect meaning; there is no arrow leading from the transformational to the semantic component.

This principle is intuitively appealing, provided that 'meaning' is interpreted as "propositional content". It says that any two, or more, sentences that have the same deep structure will necessarily have the same meaning. For example, corresponding active and passive sentences, such as 'The dog bit the postman' and 'The postman was bitten by the dog', have often been analysed as having the same deep structure. (This is shown in simplified form in Figure 4.) Most such pairs of sentences, if not all, are truth-conditionally equivalent, and therefore have the same propositional content. Arguably, however, they differ in thematic meaning, in much the same way that 'I have not read this book', 'This book I have not read', etc. differ from one another in thematic meaning (see Chapter 6). It so happens that, for syntactic reasons that do not concern us here, sets of sentences like 'I have not read this book', 'This book I have not read', etc. are given the same deep structure in the standard theory, whereas corresponding active and passive sentences are not. But this fact is irrelevant in the context of the present account. So too is the fact that much of the discussion by linguists of the relation between syntax and semantics has been confused, until recently, by the failure to distinguish

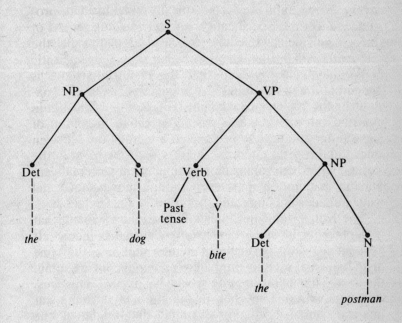

Fig. 4: Simplified representation of the deep structure of 'The dog bit the postman' and of 'The postman was bitten by the dog.'

propositional content from other kinds of sentence-meaning. The point is that some sentences will have the same deep structure, though differing quite strikingly in surface structure, and that all such sentences must be shown to have the same propositional content. This effect is achieved, simply and elegantly, by organizing the grammar in such a way that the rules of the semantic component operate solely upon deep structures.

In the Katz-Fodor theory the rules of the semantic component are usually called *projection rules*. Their purpose is twofold: (i) to distinguish meaningful from meaningless sentences; and (ii) to assign to every meaningful, or semantically well-formed, sentence a formal specification of its meaning or meanings. I will deal with these two aspects of the question separately.

We have already seen that the distinction between meaningful and meaningless sentences is not as clear-cut as it might appear at first sight (Chapter 4). And I have pointed out that, in the past, generative grammarians have tended to take too restricted a view of the semantic acceptability of sentences. In this section we are concerned with the formalization of semantic unacceptability, on the assumption that, even though it may not be as widespread as is commonly supposed, it does in fact exist.

The Katz-Fodor mechanism for handling semantic unacceptability is that of *selection restrictions*. These are associated with particular lexemes and are therefore listed, in what we may think of as dictionary entries, in the lexicon. They tell us, in effect, which pairs of lexemes can combine with one another meaningfully in various grammatical constructions. For example, they might say that the adjective 'buxom' can modify nouns like 'girl', 'woman', 'lass', etc., but not 'boy', 'man', 'lad', etc., that 'sleep' can take as its subject nouns like 'boy', 'girl', 'cat', etc., but not such nouns as 'idea' or 'quadruplicity'; and so on. If the selection restrictions are violated, the projection rules will fail to operate. Consequently, they will fail to assign to the semantically anomolous sentence a formal specification of its meaning – thereby marking the sentence as meaningless and (provided that this information is preserved in the output) indicating the nature of the anomaly.

A further task of the selection restrictions, operating in conjunction with the projection rules, is to block certain interpretations as semantically anomalous, while allowing other interpretations of the same phrases and sentences as semantically acceptable. For example, the word 'housewife' is ambiguous: in one of the senses ("housewife$_1$") it denotes a woman who keeps house; in another ("housewife$_2$") it denotes a pocket sewing kit. Many phrases in which 'housewife' is modified by an adjective ('good housewife', 'beautiful housewife', etc.) will be correspondingly ambiguous. But 'buxom housewife', presumably, will not, since "housewife$_2$", unlike "housewife$_1$", cannot combine with 'buxom'. In general, then, the selection restrictions will tend to cut down the number of interpretations assigned to lexically composite expressions. In fact, the failure to assign any interpretation at all to a sentence, referred to in the previous paragraph, can be seen as the limiting case of this process. The rules select from the meanings of an expression those, and only those, which are compatible with the (sentence-internal) context in which it occurs.

The Katz-Fodor theory of sentence-meaning is formulated within the framework of componential analysis (see Chapter 4). For example, instead of listing, in the lexical entry for 'buxom', all the other lexemes with which it can or cannot combine, the theory will identify them by means of one or more of their sense-components. It might say (in an appropriate formal notation) that 'buxom' cannot be combined, in semantically well-formed expressions, with any noun that does not have as part of its meaning the sense-components HUMAN and FEMALE. As we have seen, componential analysis runs into quite serious problems, if it is pushed beyond the proto-typical, or focal, meaning of expressions. It is for this reason that most of the textbook examples used by linguists to illustrate the operation of Katz-Fodor selection restrictions are empirically suspect. But I am not concerned, at this point, with the validity of componential analysis. Nor do I wish to take up once again the problem of drawing a distinction between contradiction and semantic anomaly. My purpose has been simply to explain what selection restrictions are and how they are formalized in the Katz-Fodor theory.

It is convenient to say something here about *categorial incongruity*, which was mentioned, though not discussed, at the end of Chapter 5. The term 'categorial incongruity' (which I have coined myself in the absence of any well-known and suitable alternative) is intended to refer to a particular kind of semantic incompatibility which is closely related to grammatical, more precisely syntactic, unacceptability. It may be introduced by means of the following examples:

'My friend existed a whole new village'

and

'My friend frightened that it was raining'.

Arguably, although I have represented them as sentences, each of them is both grammatically and semantically ill-formed. Their ungrammaticality can be readily accounted for by saying that 'exist' is an intransitive verb (and therefore cannot take an object) and that 'frighten', unlike 'think', 'say', etc., cannot occur with a *that*-clause as its object. (Such examples are handled by Chomsky in *Aspects* in terms of what he calls strict subcategorization.) The fact that they do not make sense – that they have no propositional content – can be explained by saying that it is inherent in the meaning of 'exist' that it cannot take an object, and that it is inherent in the meaning of 'frighten' that it cannot take as its object an expression referring to such abstract entities as facts or propositions. But which, if either, of these two explanations is correct?

The question is wrongly formulated. It makes unjustified assumptions about the separability of syntax and semantics. Also, it tends to distract linguists' attention from the fact that there is an intimate connection between grammatical and semantic categories and a correspondingly close, though not perfect, correlation between the syntactic and semantic structure of languages. Whether we account for categorial incongruity by means of the syntactic rules of the base component or alternatively by means of the blocking mechanism of the projection rules is of no consequence. The important point is that, whatever treatment is adopted, the details of the formalization should distinguish cases of categorial incongruity from contradictions, on the one hand, and from what are more generally handled in terms of selection restrictions, on the other.

Contradictions are meaningful, but necessarily false. Expressions whose putative anomaly results from the violation of selection restrictions can often be given a perfectly satisfactory interpretation if we are prepared to make not very radical adjustments to our assumptions about the nature of the world. Categorially incongruous expressions are meaningless and they cannot be interpreted by making minor ontological adjustments. These boundaries may be difficult to draw in respect of particular examples. But the differences are clear enough in a sufficient number of cases for the distinctions themselves to be established.

Let us now return to the Katz-Fodor projection rules. We have seen how they distinguish meaningful sentences from at least one class of meaningless, or allegedly meaningless, sentences. They also have to assign to every semantically well-formed sentence a formal specification of its meaning or meanings. Such specifications of sentence-meaning are described as *semantic representations*.

It follows from what has been said so far that a sentence will have exactly as many semantic representations as it has meanings (the limiting case being that of meaningless sentences to which the projection rules will assign no semantic representation at all). It also follows that sentences with the same deep structure will have the same semantic representation. The converse, however, does not follow; in the standard theory of transformational-generative grammar (in contrast with so-called generative semantics, one of its alternatives), sentences that differ in deep structure may nevertheless have the same meaning. This is a consequence of the existence of synonymous, but lexically distinct, expressions (see Chapter 2) and of the way in which lexicalization is handled in the standard theory. We may simply note that this is so, without going into the details.

But what precisely are semantic representations? And how are they constructed by the projection rules? These two questions are, of course, interdependent (by virtue of the principle of compositionality). A semantic representation is a collection, or amalgamation, of sense-components. But it is not merely an unstructured set of such components. As we saw in Chapter 4, it is not generally possible to formalize the meaning of individual lexemes in set-theoretic terms. It is even more obviously the case that sentence-meaning cannot be formalized in this way. If a semantic representation were nothing more than a set of sense-components (or semantic markers, in Katz-Fodor terminology), any two sentences containing exactly the same lexemes would be assigned the same semantic representation. For example, 'The dog bit the postman' and 'The postman bit the dog', and indefinitely many pairs of sentences like them, would be given the same representations. This is patently incorrect. What is required is some formalization of semantic representations that will preserve the semantically relevant syntactic distinctions of deep structure.

It is probably fair to say that in the years that have passed since the publication of 'The structure of a semantic theory' by Katz and Fodor little real progress has been made along these lines. The formalization has been complicated by the introduction of a variety of technical devices. But no general solution has been found to the problem of deciding exactly how many projection rules are needed and how they differ formally one from another. The process whereby the meanings of lexemes are *amalgamated* to form syntactically structured complexes of allegedly universal sense-components is still presented in essentially set-theoretic terms.

Meanwhile, the whole concept of semantic representations has been challenged, on two grounds, by logicians and philosophers. First of all, they have pointed out that Katz-Fodor semantic representations make use of what is in effect a formal language and that the vocabulary-units of this language (conventionally written in small capitals, as in Chapter 4) stand in need of interpretation. This objection may be countered, more or less plausibly, by saying that the formal language in question is the allegedly universal language of thought, which we all know by virtue of being human. The second challenge to the notion of semantic representation comes from those who argue that they are unnecessary; that everything done satisfactorily by means of semantic representations can be done no less satisfactorily without them – by means of rules of inference operating in conjunction with meaning postulates. It is perhaps too early to predict that this approach will be more successful than the Katz-Fodor theory has been. But it does avoid many of the difficulties, empirical and theoretical, associated with componential analysis. And many of those who advocate it have declared their preference for Montague grammar, to which we now turn.

Montague grammar

What is commonly referred to as Montague grammar is a particular approach to the analysis of natural languages initiated by the American logician Richard Montague in the late 1960s and early 1970s. In the last few years it has been adopted by an increasing number of linguists – many of them converts, as it were, from Chomskyan tranformational-generative grammar – and is now the object of intensive research. (Montague himself died when he was still quite young, in 1971.)

Some of the differences between Montague grammar and the Katz-Fodor theory are a matter of historical accident. Montague's work is more firmly rooted in formal semantics than the Katz-Fodor theory is and gives proportionately less consideration to many topics that have been at the forefront of the linguist's attention. In fact, 'grammar' for Montague included only part of what the standard theory of generative grammar sets out to cover. There is nothing in Montague's own work about phonological representation or inflection. As a logician, he may have underestimated both the complexity and the theoretical interest of these branches of linguistics. The Katz-Fodor theory, on the other hand, finds its place (as Figure 3 indicates) within a more comprehensive theory of the structure of languages, in which semantics and phonology are on equal terms. Linguists who have adopted Montague grammar are well aware of the necessity of integrating phonology and morphology with syntax and, either directly or indirectly, with semantics.

More interesting is the status of transformational rules, on the one hand, and of componential analysis, or lexical decomposition, on the other. Montague himself did not make use of transformational rules. There were at least three reasons for this. First, the syntactic rules that he used in what we may think of as the base component of his grammar are more powerful than Chomskyan phrase-structure rules. Second, he was not particularly concerned to block the generation of syntactically ill-formed strings of words, as long as they could be characterized as ill-formed by the rules of semantic interpretation. Third, he had a preference for bringing the semantic analysis of sentences into as close a correspondence as possible with their surface structure. There is therefore no such thing as deep structure in Montague's own system. But this is not inherent in Montague grammar as such; and a number of linguists have made proposals for the addition of a transformational component to the system. At the same time, it must also be noted that the role of transformational rules has been successively reduced in Chomskyan transformational-generative grammar over the last ten years or so. Montague's position no longer seems as eccentric and as badly motivated to generative grammarians as it may once have done.

As for componential analysis, much the same remarks can be made here too. Montague grammar as such is not incompatible, in principle, with the decomposition, or factorization, of lexical meaning into sense-components. Indeed, one or two linguists have made proposals for the incorporation of rules for lexical decomposition within the general framework of Montague grammar. But as I have mentioned in the previous section and in Chapter 4, componential analysis is not as widely accepted by linguists now as it was in the 1960s and early 1970s.

The main point I want to make here is that the comparison of Chomskyan generative grammar with Montague grammar is complicated for the non-specialist by the fact that some of the differences between them derive from purely historical circumstances. Unfortunately, most presentations of Montague grammar are highly technical. And most accounts of Chomskyan generative grammar, whether technical or non-technical, fail to draw the distinction between what is essential to it and what is, or was at the time of writing, currently accepted opinion.

Of course, Montague grammar is of its nature a very technical subject (just as Chomskyan generative grammar is). It would be foolish to encourage the belief that any real understanding of the details can be achieved unless one has a considerable facility in mathematical logic. However, it is not the details that are of concern here – and I should soon be out of my depth if they were! My purpose is simply to explain, non-technically, some of the most important characteristics of Montague grammar, insofar as they are relevant to the formalization of sentence-meaning.

Montague semantics – the semantic component of a Montague grammar – is resolutely truth-conditional. Its applicability is restricted, in principle, to the propositional content of sentences. Just how big a restriction this turns out to be in practice depends upon one's evaluation of the points made in the previous chapter. Most of the advocates of Montague semantics are probably committed to the view that the whole of sentence-meaning is explicable, ultimately, in terms of propositional content. It is generally recognized, however, that non-declarative sentences, on the one hand, and non-indicative sentences, on the other, are problematical from this point of view. Attempts have been made to handle such sentences within the framework of Montague grammar. I shall say nothing about these here or about the other phenomena discussed in the previous chapter. ·

Unlike certain other truth-conditional theories, Montague semantics operates, not with a concept of absolute truth, but with a particular notion of relative truth: truth under an interpretation or, alternatively, in the technical terminology of model theory (which need not be explained here), truth-in-a-model. What model theory does in effect is to formalize the distinction that I drew earlier between propositions and propositional content. It does this by drawing upon the distinction between *extension* and *intension* (mentioned in Chapter 2) and relating this to a particular notion of *possible worlds*, which originated (as we saw in Chapter 4) with Leibniz.

The traditional distinction between extension and intension has been exploited in a variety of ways in modern logic and formal semantics, so that the term 'intensional' (not to be confused with its homophone 'intentional') has a quite bewildering range of interconnected uses. I will restrict myself to what is of immediate relevance.

We may begin by identifying Frege's distinction between reference (Bedeutung) and sense (Sinn) with the distinction between extension and intension. We can then extend this distinction, as Frege did, to the analysis of sentence-meaning; we can say that the sense, or intension, of a sentence is its propositional content, whereas its reference, or extension, is its truth-value (on particular occasions of utterance). Most people at first find it strange that Frege, and following him many, though not all, formal semanticists, should have taken sentences (or propositions) to refer to truth or falsity, rather than to the situations that they purport to describe. But this view of the matter has certain formal advantages with respect to compositionality.

The next step is to invoke the notion of possible worlds. According to Leibniz, as we saw earlier, necessarily true (or false) propositions are propositions that are true (or false) in all possible worlds. The notion has also been applied, in an intuitively plausible way, in the definition of descriptive synonymy, as follows: expressions are descripttively synonymous if, and only if, they have the same extension in all possible worlds. Since expressions are descriptively synonymous if, and only if, they have the same sense (which we have identified with their intension), it follows that the intension of an expression is either its extension in all possible worlds or some function which determines its extension in all possible worlds. The second of these alternatives is the one that is adopted in Montague grammar. The intension of an expression, we are told, is a function from possible worlds to extensions. But what does this mean?

It is perhaps easier to approach the question from a psychological, or conceptualist, point of view. A world, let us say, is a set of entities. Foremost among these are what I will call first-order entities – persons, animals and other animate and inanimate physical objects. These are located in space-time (i.e., at any particular time they are in a particular place) and they may be involved, singly or jointly, in various static or dynamic situations. For example, John may be in love with Mary; Peter may be giving a book to Veronica; a particular herd of cows may be grazing in a particular field; and so on. Since many of these situations are dynamic, and entities are disappearing or coming into existence all the time, the world itself is not the same from one moment to the next. We normally express this fact by saying that the world is constantly changing from one state to another. It would be just as reasonable to treat this succession of world-states as a set of worlds replacing one another through time. Only one of these worlds is the actual world at any one time. But they are all possible worlds, some of which have been actualized in the past, others of which are to be actualized in the future.

Every natural language provides its users with (a) the means of identifying the world that is actual at the time of speaking and distinguishing it from past and future worlds, and (b) the means of referring to individual entities and sets of entities in whatever world has been identified. Let us refer to whatever means is used to identify worlds (tense, adverbs of time, etc.) as an *index* to the world in question. I shall have more to say about this in Chapter 10: here I will simply draw the reader's attention to the connection between the term 'index', as I have just used it, and 'indexicality'. An alternative to 'index', in this sense, is 'point of reference': possible worlds are identified from a particular point of reference.

Granted that we can identify the world in question, how do we know what is being referred to by the expression that is used, when a sentence is uttered? For example, how do we know what 'those cows' refers to in the utterance of 'Those cows are Guernseys'. The traditional answer, as we have seen, is that we know the concept "cow" and that this, being the intension of 'cow', determines its extension. (We also need to be able to interpret the demonstrative pronoun 'that' and the grammatical category of plurality. But we may neglect this here.) Concepts are often explained in terms of pictures or images, as in certain versions of the ideational theory of meaning (see Chapter 1). But we can now think of them more generally, as functions: that is, as rules, or operations, which assign a unique value to the members of their domain. It is as if we had a book of rules for all the expressions in the language (the rules being their intensions) and that we identified the extension of any given expression in any particular world (the domain of the function) by looking up the rule (or function) and applying it to the world. This rule, then, is a function from possible worlds to an extension: it picks out from the world that is its domain the set of entities that are being referred to; and this set is the value of the function.

But we do not have, and in principle cannot have, a list of rules in our heads for all the expressions in a language. Apart from any other psychological considerations that would render this hypothesis implausible, there is the fact, mentioned in an earlier section of this chapter, that natural languages contains infinitely many expressions. And competent users of such languages are able, by virtue of their competence, to produce and interpret arbitrarily selected members of these infinite sets of expressions. What is required, then, is yet another function (or set of functions), which determines the intension of composite expressions on the basis of the intension of basic expressions (lexemes) and of the syntactic rules (the rules of composition) which generate them.

All I have done here, of course, is to reformulate Frege's principle of compositionality within an intensional framework. As I said earlier, I have been taking the principle of compositionality to apply primarily to sense, and only derivatively to reference. (Reference is mediated in this respect by denotation and context – in a way that is in part explained by what has just been said and will be further explained, informally, in later chapters.)

It is at this point that Montague grammar comes into its own. Montague sought to establish a much closer correspondence between syntax and semantics than the standard theory of transformational-generative grammar does. He achieved this, insofar as he was successful, by adopting a particular kind of *categorial* grammar and by putting the categories of syntax (roughly comparable with the major categories and subcategories of traditional grammar: noun-phrases, nouns, predicates, intransitive verbs, transitive verbs, adverbs, etc.) into one-to-one correspondence with intensional categories.

We will not go into the details of categorial grammar or of the mechanism whereby the correspondence between syntactic and semantic, or intensional, categories is established. All that needs to be said is that a categorial grammar is a particularly elegant kind of grammar, which derives all the other syntactic categories from the basic categories of noun-phrase and sentence. The term 'categorial' reflects the philosophical origins of this kind of grammar in the work of the German philosopher Edmund Husserl (1859–1938) – the founder of phenomenology. But categorial grammar as such is no more closely associated with one kind of ontology (Aristotelian, Kantian, phenomenological) than it is with another. It does rest, however, upon the principle of *categorial congruity*, to which I referred earlier (and this is why I used the term 'categorial' in this connection): the principle of syntactic and semantic interdependence with respect to the rules of composition. This notion of congruity is eminently traditional.

So far, I have restricted the discussion to possible worlds that differ from the actual world only in that they have been actualized in the past or will be actualized in the future. But there is no need to maintain this restriction. Indeed, the real pay-off from the formalization of possible worlds by Montague and others comes from the fact that it enables us to handle, in a logically respectable way, statements about worlds that we know will never be actualized: the worlds of our dreams, hopes and fears; the worlds of science-fiction, drama, and make-believe. I will come back to this point, in connection with the notion of epistemic modality, in Chapter 10. At this stage, it will be sufficient to note that Montague grammar, though still in its infancy, has been more successful than previous formal systems constructed by logicians for the semantic analysis of natural languages.

In particular, it handles, in an intuitively satisfying way, a range of well-known problems is philosophical semantics: the fact that in certain so-called intensional contexts the substitution of expressions with the same extension affects truth-conditionality (e.g., 'I want to meet the first woman prime minister of Great Britain' and 'I want to meet Margaret Thatcher', in the intensional interpretation, have different truth-conditions); the fact that expressions may lack an extension entirely and yet not be synonymous (e.g., 'unicorn' and 'centaur'); and so on. Granted, these may not be problems which, of themselves, cause the man in the street, or even the linguist, to lose sleep. But they are all connected with the more general problem of formulating, as precisely as possible, the principles whereby we are able to assign interpretations to expressions according to the context in which they are used and to identify the referents of referring expressions.

In what has been said about possible worlds so far in this section, I have for simplicity adopted a psychological, or conceptualist, point of view: I have talked as if it is the aim of formal semantics to construct models of the mental representations that human beings have of the external world. Looked at from this point of view, a proposition is true or false of the actual or non-actual world that is represents according to whether it is *in correspondence with* that world or not. This is a perfectly legitimate way of talking about formal semantics, and it is one that is favoured by many psychologists, linguists and computer scientists interested in artificial intelligence. But it is not the one that is customarily adopted by logicians and philosophers. There are, in fact, several philosophically different ways in which the term 'possible world' can be interpreted.

Indeed, the reader may well have noticed that I have not been absolutely consistent in my own use of the term. Just now I have talked of propositions as being true or false *of* the world that they represent; elsewhere I have said that propositions are true or false *in* a world, tautologies being true, and contradictions false, in all possible worlds. Arguably, it is more in line with everyday conceptions and with traditional usage of the term 'proposition' to say that propositions represent, or describe, a world, rather than that they are, in some sense, in it. However, many philosophers and logicians have adopted the second way of talking. Without going further into this question, I will simply note that some formal semanticists have explicitly defined a possible world to be a set of propositions, while others have said that a proposition is the set of worlds in which, or of which, it is true. For purely logical purposes it makes little difference which of these views we adopt, though the choice between them may be motivated by broader philosophical considerations.

It would be impossible, and inappropriate in a book of this kind, to go into all the philosophical ramifications of the adoption of one view of possible worlds, and propositions, rather than another. In conclusion, however, I should like to emphasize that model-theoretic, or indexical, semantics provides us, at least in principle, with the means of formalizing many of the phenomena found in natural languages that are not satisfactorily formalized in earlier systems of formal semantics. For example, it enables us to formalize various relations of *accessibility* holding between different possible worlds. To take just one aspect of this: there is an intuitively clear sense in which, in the everyday use of language, we normally operate with the assumption that the past, but not the future, is accessible to us. And this assumption is built into the structure of the system of tenses and moods in many, if not all, languages. Indexical semantics can handle phenomena of this kind. More generally, it allows us to formalize the fact that a speaker is constrained by certain kinds of accessibility in the selection, or construction, of the possible worlds that he refers to and in the way that he refers to them; and also of the fact that he necessarily refers to the world that he is describing from the viewpoint of the world that he is in. These two facts, as we shall see in Chapter 10, are crucial for any proper treatment of indexicality and modality in natural languages.

Summary

In this chapter, we have been concerned with the formalization of sentence-meaning. We have concentrated more particularly upon the Katz-Fodor theory, which originated in Chomskyan generative grammar, and Montague's system of formal semantics, which is now being advocated by an increasing number of linguists, as well as logicians. One of the strengths of Montague grammar, as we have seen, is its ability to handle the phenomenon of indexicality and the intuitively attractive notion of possible worlds. We return to this question in Chapter 10. Meanwhile, we must broaden our horizons and look at various aspects of natural-language meaning which derive from the context of utterance.

PART 4

Beyond the Sentence: Utterances and Texts

8 *Words and Deeds*

The theory of speech acts

'Words are also deeds.'
Ralph Waldo Emerson, *The Poet*

So far, we have dealt mainly with a view of meaning in language which assumes that languages are simply sets of sentences: and we have given priority to sentences that are used to make descriptive statements, which may be either true or false. This is clearly a very limited view, both of language and of meaning, and one that has been much criticized.

One of the most influential critics in recent years was the Oxford philosopher, J.L. Austin (1911–60), whose ideas have been much discussed, not only by philosophers, but also by linguists, psychologists, literary critics and representatives of many other disciplines. In this chapter, we use his views as a departure-point for showing how one might go beyond the treatment of a language as if it were no more than a set of descriptive statements.

Utterances

The term 'utterance', as I pointed out in Chapter 1, is ambiguous. It can be used to refer either to the process of uttering or to the products of a process. Utterances in the first of these two senses are commonly called *speech acts*; utterances in the second sense may be described as *inscriptions*. It is one of my principal aims in this chapter to clarify the relation between speech acts and inscriptions and, in doing so, to develop in more detail the distinction between sentence-meaning and utterance-meaning. I will operate, as far as possible, with Austin's terminology and conceptual framework. But I shall need to add one or two distinctions of my own, in order to make more precise than Austin and his followers have done the rather complex relation that holds between speech acts and sentences.

Actually, the term 'speech act' itself is somewhat misleading. Apart from anything else, it throws too much emphasis upon that part of the production of utterances which results in their inscription in the physical medium of sound. 'Language act' would be a much better term. Since 'speech act' is now widely employed in the technical sense that Austin gave to it, I will make no attempt to replace it. It must constantly be borne in mind, however, that 'speech act', like 'utterance', on the one hand, and 'inscription' or 'text', on the other, is intended to cover the production of both written and spoken language. The distinctions that I have just drawn are summarized in Figure 5, which also includes a reminder that 'speech act' is to be understood throughout in the sense of 'language act'.

Austin

Austin himself never presented a fully developed theory of speech acts. The nearest he came to doing so was in the William James lectures, which were delivered at Harvard in 1955 and published, after his death, as *How to Do Things With Words* (1962). Austin had been lecturing on the same topic for some years previously in Oxford and had delivered papers relating to it as early as 1940, but did not leave behind him a fully revised and publishable manuscript of his William James lectures. It is hardly surprising, therefore, that there is no agreed and definitive version of the theory of speech acts. Indeed, it is not

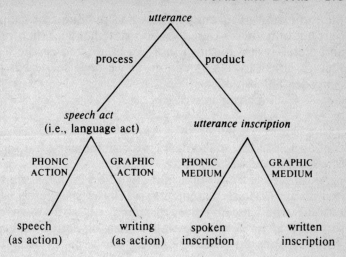

Fig. 5

clear that Austin was even trying to construct a theory of speech acts, in the sense in which the term 'theory' is interpreted by many of those who have taken up his ideas. He belonged to a school of philosophy, whose members tended to be suspicious of formalization and the drawing of sharp distinctions.

Austin's main purpose, originally at least, was to challenge what he regarded as the descriptive fallacy: the view that the only philosophically interesting function of language was that of making true or false statements. More specifically, he was attacking the verificationist thesis, associated with logical positivism, that sentences were meaningful if and only if they expressed verifiable, or falsifiable, propositions. We have already looked at verificationism in connection with the notion of truth-conditionality (Chapter 5). It will be recalled that, when Austin first concerned himself with the question, the verificationists had already had to face the objection that their criterion of meaningfulness had the effect of ruling out, not only the so-called pseudo-statements of theology and metaphysics, but also those of ethics and aesthetics. One response to this objection, as we have seen, was to concede that sentences like

'Cannibalism is wrong'

or

'Monet is better than Manet'

cannot be used to make descriptive statements, but only to express one's feelings.

Another was to say that, although they can be used to make true or false statements, what the speaker is describing when he makes such statements is his own or someone else's attitudes, rather than objective reality. What Austin did in his relatively early papers was to criticise the second of these alternatives. He subsequently pointed out that many more of our everyday utterances are pseudo-statements than either the verificationists or their opponents had realized. For example, according to Austin, if I utter the sentence

'I promise to pay you £5',

with the purpose of making a promise (and of communicating to my addressee the fact that I am making a promise), I am not saying something, true or false, about my state of mind, but committing myself to a particular course of action.

This, in brief, is the philosophical context in which Austin first put forward his now famous distinction between *constative* and *performative* utterances. A constative utterance is, by definition, a statement-making utterance. (Austin prefers 'constative' to 'descriptive', because "not all true or false statements are descriptions". For our purposes, the two terms may be treated as equivalent.) Performative utterances, in contrast, are those in the production of which the speaker, or writer, performs an act of doing rather than saying.

This distinction between saying and doing (reflected in the title of Austin's Oxford lectures, 'Words and Deeds', which I have borrowed as a general heading for this chapter) was eventually abandoned. However, the distinction between constative and non-constative utterances was not. It is simply that, in the latest version that we have of Austin's own work, constative utterances are presented as but one class of performatives. Similarly, saying – in the special sense of saying that something is or is not the case – is seen as a particular kind of doing. And, as we shall see, Austin goes into the question of saying and doing in considerable detail. In fact, this is what Austin's theory of speech acts, insofar as it is a theory, is all about. It is a theory of pragmatics (in the etymological sense of 'pragmatics': "the study of action, or doing"). Furthermore, it is a theory of social pragmatics: a theory of saying as doing within the framework of social institutions and conventions. This aspect of Austin's theory has not always been given the emphasis that it deserves.

A second distinction that Austin draws is between *explicit* and *primary* performatives. This applies, in principle, to both constative and non-constative utterances. We shall return to this later. For the present, we can say that an explicit performative is one in which the utterance-inscription contains an expression that makes explicit what kind of act is being performed. This definition will need to be refined in several respects. As it stands, it is perhaps broader than Austin intended, and yet narrower than it ought to be. But it certainly covers all the examples that Austin and his followers have used to illustrate the class of explicit performatives. In particular, it covers non-constative utterances of

'I promise to pay you £5'.

Such sentences contain a so-called performative verb, and it is this verb, 'promise', together with the fact that it has a first-person subject and is in the simple present indicative form, which makes explicit the nature of the speech act that is being performed when the sentence is uttered in order to make a promise.

Of course, one can make a promise without doing so by means of an explicit performative. For example, one can make a promise by uttering

'I will pay you £5'.

In this case, one will have produced what Austin refers to as a primary (i.e., non-explicit) performative. This is non-explicit, in terms of the definition given above, in that there is no expression in the utterance-inscription itself (*I'll pay you £5*) which makes explicit the fact that it is to be taken as a promise rather than a prediction or a statement.

This will serve as a sufficient, though informal and rather imprecise, account of what Austin had in mind when he drew his distinction between explicit and primary performatives. It will be noted that it is utterances, not sentences, that are classified as being constative or non-constative, and as being either explicitly performative or not. When linguists use the term 'performative sentence' they are usually referring to sentences like 'I promise to pay you £5', which contain a so-called performative verb and are commonly uttered as explicitly non-constative utterances.

In what follows I will make use of several of Austin's terms. But I will not always give them exactly the same interpretation as he gave them. In some instances, Austin's own interpretation is far from clear; in others, it is clear enough, but controversial. There is the further problem that Austin's view of the distinction between sentences and utterances was very different from the one that I have adopted in this book. I will therefore re-interpret what Austin has to say about *locutionary act* – a particular kind of speech act – in the light of this distinction.

The reader is reminded at this point that I am drawing a systematic notational distinction between utterance-inscriptions and sentences: italics for the former and single quotation-marks for the latter. It is important to maintain the distinction, conceptually if not notationally, even in the case of those utterance-inscriptions that would normally be regarded as sentences. Thus, 'I will pay you £5' is a sentence which may be uttered, in either speech or writing, as *I will pay you £5* or alternatively (with contraction of *I will*) as *I'll pay you £5*, both of which would normally be classified as sentences by linguists.

Locutionary acts

To perform a locutionary act is to produce an utterance-inscription with a particular form and a more or less determinate meaning.

Most of the utterance-inscriptions that we produce in everyday conversation – i.e., most of the products of our locutionary acts – are not sentences. Some of them are ungrammatical; some are grammatical, but elliptical (e.g., *Been here long?*, *Nice weather for the time of year*, etc.); some are neither grammatical nor ungrammatical; yet others, of course, are both ungrammatical and unacceptable – resulting from inattention, lapses of memory or malfunctioning of one kind or another in the actual production of language-signals.

Since we are deliberately restricting our attention, for the time being, to utterance-inscriptions that would be classified grammatically as sentences, we can temporarily ignore much of the complexity that a fuller discussion of locutionary acts will require. In particular, we can temporarily assume that to perform a locutionary act is necessarily to utter a sentence. However, it is important at this point to note that two people can utter the same sentence without necessarily saying the same thing, and they can say the same thing without necessarily uttering the same sentence.

In fact, there are various ways in which one can interpret the everyday expression 'say the same thing'. Austin's theory of speech acts can be seen as addressing itself to this issue and as explicating the several senses of the verb 'say' in which saying is doing. Let us begin by noting that the following sentence is ambiguous, according to whether the verb 'say' is taken as meaning "assert" or "utter":

'John and Mary said the same thing'.

Under one interpretation, it has much the same truth-conditions, and therefore the same propositional content, as

'John and Mary asserted the same proposition'.

Under the other, it may be paraphrased, in the technical metalanguage that we have been building up, as

'John and Mary produced the same utterance-inscription'.

It is also worth noting that, although 'thing' is not similarly ambiguous, there is a striking and theoretically important difference between one class of things and another. Propositions, as we have seen, are abstract entities of a particular kind. Utterance-inscriptions, on the other hand, have physical properties, which are identifiable by means of one or more of the senses: hearing, sight, touch, etc.

It is clear from what has been said in earlier chapters that it is possible to assert the same proposition by uttering different sentences. They might be sentences of different languages: e.g., English 'It is raining', French 'Il pleut' and German 'Es regnet'. They might be sentences of the same language, such as corresponding actives and passives: e.g., 'The dog bit the postman' and 'The postman was bitten by the dog'. Conversely, as we saw in Chapter 7, one can assert different propositions by uttering the same sentence in different contexts and by assigning different values to the referring expressions that it contains. (For example, 'My friend is waiting for me' expresses indefinitely many propositions according to the value assigned to 'my friend', 'I' and the tense of the verb.)

We have noted, then, that there is an important distinction to be drawn between the utterance of sentences and

the assertion of propositions. There is also a distinction to be drawn between the utterance of sentences and the production of utterance-inscriptions. This can be shown by means of a few simple examples. Let us suppose that John says
>*I'll meet you at the bank*

and Mary says
>*I'll meet you at the bank.*

Or, again, that they both say
>*Flying planes can be dangerous.*

We can readily agree that in one sense of 'say', in each instance, they have said the same thing: they have produced the same utterance-inscription. (More precisely, they have produced tokens of the same utterance-type.) Let us also agree that what they have uttered is, in each case, a sentence. But have they both uttered the same sentence? It is important to realize that we cannot answer this question without knowing not only what forms have been uttered, but also of what expressions they are forms. If *bank* in John's utterance-inscription is a form of 'bank$_1$' (meaning "financial institution") and *bank* in Mary's is a form of 'bank$_2$' (meaning "side of a river, etc."), they have uttered different sentences. Similarly, if *flying* in John's utterance-inscription is a form of the intransitive verb 'to fly' (so that 'flying planes' means roughly "planes which are flying") and *flying* in Mary's is a form of the corresponding transitive verb 'fly' (so that 'flying planes' means roughly "to fly planes"), they have once again uttered different sentences.

The fact that one can produce the same utterance-inscription without having uttered the same sentence is obscured in a good deal of recent work in semantics and pragmatics by the looseness with which the terms 'sentence' and 'utterance' are employed. It is arguable that Austin, too, fell victim to the failure to draw a sufficiently sharp distinction between sentences and utterances. But he was certainly aware of the point that has just been illustrated; and he had a more sophisticated understanding of the complexity of the relation between sentences and utterance-inscriptions than many of his followers appear to have. For the analysis that he himself gives of locutionary acts, unclear though it is in certain respects and technically defective in others, certainly depends upon his recognition of the fact that phonetically identical utterance-inscriptions can differ in terms of their constituent expressions and grammatical structure.

This leads to an additional point: phonetic identity is not a necessary condition of the identity of utterance-inscriptions. If we ask Mary to repeat John's utterance of *It's raining* or *I'll meet you at the bank*, we do not expect her to mimic his voice-quality or to reproduce such paralinguistic features as rhythm and tempo. We do not even expect her to imitate John's accent, though it might differ strikingly from her own. For example, if John is a working-class Londoner with a Cockney accent and Mary is an upper-class lady from New England, they will pronounce *It's raining* and almost every other potential utterance-inscription of English in characteristically different ways. And yet in many cases, if not all, pairs of phonetically distinct utterance-inscriptions will be identified by native speakers as *tokens* of the same *type*.

This shows that phonetic identity is not a necessary condition of the type-token identity of utterance-inscriptions. It also illustrates the point that the type-token identity of utterances is, up to a point, theory-independent: it can be established in particular instances without reference to one theory of language-structure rather than another. But theory-independence, in this sense, breaks down in respect of the intonation-contour of utterances. It simply is not clear, in everyday life, whether two intonationally distinct pronunciations of *It's raining* or *I'll meet you at the bank* would count as tokens of the same type. In both cases there is room for debate as to whether stress and intonation are relevant or not. For simplicity of exposition, however, I will here take the view that for two people to produce the same utterance-inscription it is sufficient for them to utter what they and others will recognise as the same string of forms, regardless of the intonation-contour and stress-pattern that are superimposed upon it. And I will take the same view as far as sentences are concerned.

For example, if John says *It's raining* with falling intonation and a neutral stress-pattern whereas Mary says *It's raining* with emphatic stress and rising intonation on the form *raining*, I will declare them, not only to have produced the same utterance-inscription, but also to have uttered the same sentence: 'It is raining.' (It will be noted that I also count the contraction of *it is* to *it's*, and all similar phenomena, as irrelevant to the type-token identity of utterance-inscriptions.) This is not so much a matter of fact as of theoretical and methodological decision. Many linguists would disagree, on theoretical grounds, with the view that I have taken here. But few linguists, so far, have given serious attention to the question; and much of what appears to be genuine disagreement might turn out to be purely terminological.

We can now split the performance of a locutionary act into two logically independent parts: (i) the production of an inscription in some appropriate physical medium; and (ii) the construction of such and such a sentence. They are logically independent, because the same inscription can be associated with two or more quite different sentences and, conversely, the same sentence can be associated with two or more quite different inscriptions. Using Austin's terms, we can say that a locutionary act is the product of (i) a *phonic* act of producing an inscription (in the phonic medium of sound); and (ii) a *phatic* act of constructing a particular sentence in a particular language. The first of these two acts is, of course, dependent upon the use of one medium rather than another. The production of utterance-inscriptions in some non-phonic medium – notably when we are writing, rather than speaking – will involve non-phonic acts of one kind or another. As I said earlier, the term 'speech act' should not be interpreted as applying only to the production of spoken utterances. The same goes for the term 'locutionary act'.

We have not yet finished with the analysis of locutionary acts; we still have to reckon with the fact that sentences are uttered in particular contexts and that part of the meaning of the resultant utterance-inscription derives from the context in which it is produced. This is notably the case in respect of the reference of the referring expressions that it contains; and reference, as we have seen in Part 3, is a part of utterance-meaning, not sentence-meaning. The third component of the locutionary act, which includes the assignment of reference and may be described more generally as contextualization, is what Austin calls the *rhetic* act.

I shall make no further use of Austin's terms 'phonic', 'phatic' and 'rhetic'. They are not widely employed in the literature; and I have, in any case, given them a somewhat different interpretation from the one that Austin himself did. What is important is the tripartite analysis itself, which depends, as we have seen, partly on the distinction between language and medium and partly on the distinction between sentences and utterance-inscriptions.

It may be worth adding, in view of the fairly general confusion and misunderstanding that exists in this respect, that the distinction between sentences and utterance-inscriptions is not simply a distinction between types and tokens. This follows from the fact that two utterance-inscriptions produced on different occasions can be identified as tokens of the same type without knowing what sentences have been uttered. Furthermore, as I have emphasized in this section, tokens of the same utterance-inscription can result from the utterance of different sentences; and, conversely, tokens of different utterance-inscriptions can be produced by uttering one and the same sentence on different occasions.

This point is crucial for any theory of language-structure that operates with a more or less traditional notion of the sentence. We want to be able to say, for example, that tokens of the following utterance-inscriptions, whether spoken or written:

   I have

result from the utterance of indefinitely many sentences, including

   'I have done the washing up'
   'I have been to California'
   'I have (got) an electric typewriter'.

Conversely, we want to be able to say that a sentence like

   'I have done the washing up'

can be uttered, not only as

   I have done the washing up

but also as

   I have done it
   I have
   Me

(with some appropriate prosodic contour, if these utterances are inscribed in the phonic medium). As we shall see in Chapter 9, the analysis of locutionary acts outlined in this section enables us to make statements like these in a way that is both theoretically and empirically satisfying. But first, having explained in some detail what is involved in the performance of a locutionary act, we must look at what is generally regarded as Austin's most original contribution to the study of meaning: his development of the notion of illocutionary force.

Illocutionary force

Saying is doing. But there are distinguishable senses of the verb 'say'. In one sense, it means, roughly, "utter" or, more technically, "perform a locutionary act". As we have just seen, saying in this sense of the verb involves three different kinds of doing:

(i)   the act of producing an inscription;
(ii) the act of composing a sentence;
(iii) the act of contextualizing that sentence.

To utter a sentence, in all normal circumstances, is to perform a complex act in which these three kinds of doing are integrated and have as their product some identifiable and meaningful language-signal: an utterance-inscription.

There is yet another sense of 'say' in which, as I have already pointed out, it is possible for two people to say the same thing without performing the same locutionary act and without uttering the same sentence. They can say that something is, or is not, the case: that is, they can assert the same proposition. For example, let us suppose that John says (or writes)

> *Peter is mad*

and Mary, on some other occasion, says (or writes)

> *Your brother is mad.*

Let us further suppose that 'Peter' and 'your brother' refer to the same person and that 'mad' is being used with the same sense (rather than on one occasion with the meaning "insane" and on the other with the meaning "angry"). Provided that they have indeed asserted a proposition, John and Mary will have asserted the same proposition, and will therefore have said the same thing in this other sense of 'say'. But they will not necessarily have made an assertion.

To make an assertion, or statement, is not to perform a locutionary act of one kind rather than another; it is to perform that locutionary act with one kind of *illocutionary force*, rather than another. According to Austin, as we have seen, the constative or descriptive function of language is only one of its functions. We also use language to ask questions, issue commands and make promises; to threaten, insult and cajole; and, of course, to do all those things for which Austin originally employed the term 'performative' – to baptize a child into the Christian faith, to plight one's troth, to sentence a convicted criminal, and so on. In short, there are many different language-functions and correspondingly many different kinds of illocutionary force.

But how many? One way of tackling this question is to

ask how many verbs in a particular language can be used in explicitly performative utterances, as 'promise', for example, can be used non-constatively in the utterance of
  'I promise to pay you £5'.
There are hundreds, if not thousands, of such verbs in English. Some of them are more or less synonymous: e.g., 'implore' and 'beseech'. Others, though obviously not synonymous, can be seen intuitively as falling into classes with common characteristics. For example, 'promise' and 'undertake' are semantically related in that, when they are used in explicitly performative utterances, their use commits the speaker to a particular course of action. All such verbs, and therefore the particular kinds of illocutionary force which they serve to make explicit, may be grouped together as members of one class. Similarly for other sets of semantically related performative verbs: e.g., 'order', 'command', 'request', etc., all of which have the common property that, when they are used in explicitly performative utterances, their use expresses the speaker's will that some other person, usually the addressee, should carry out a particular course of action.

Austin himself provided the outlines of one classificatory scheme of this kind at the very end of *How to Do Things With Words*. Other such schemes, differing to a greater or lesser extent from Austin's, have since been put forward by his followers. The very fact that alternative more or less plausible classifications are possible constitutes a problem. How do we decide between one classification and another? There is no reason to suppose that the set of performative verbs in English or any other language will distinguish all possible kinds of illocutionary force. There is still less reason to suppose that there must be some uniquely correct analysis of such verbs, applicable to all cultures and to all languages. Indeed, the vast majority of performative verbs in English and other languages are obviously culture-dependent. For example, the meaning and use of the verb 'swear', insofar as it differs from that of 'promise' and 'undertake', on the one hand, or 'covenant', 'contract' and 'guarantee', on the other, depends upon the culturally established institution of the taking of oaths.

Moreover, nowadays it is becoming clear that it may be wrong to attach particular importance to performative verbs. Admittedly, they had a special status in Austin's original formulation of the distinction between constative and performative utterances. But this was because at that time he was mainly concerned with the descriptive fallacy and, looked at from this point of view, sentences like

'I promise to pay you £5'

were obviously of greater theoretical interest than sentences like

'I will pay you £5'.

In terms of the later, more general, notion of illocutionary force, we have no grounds for confining our attention to declarative sentences containing performative verbs.

It is also worth noting at this point that the definition of 'explicit performative' which I gave earlier in this chapter ("one in which the utterance-inscription contains an expression that makes explicit what kind of act is being performed") makes no reference to performative verbs as such. For example, the expression 'by Heaven' might be used by members of a particular group of English speakers as an equally explicit alternative to the use of the verb 'swear', in order to indicate that they are taking an oath. In which case, in the appropriate circumstances

By Heaven, I'll pay you £5

would count as an explicit performative. It is but a short step to the recognition of the further possibility that a speaker should be able to make explicit the illocutionary force of this utterance, not by using a particular expression, but by using a particular modal particle, a particular grammatical mood or, even, a particular intonation-pattern. I will come back to this.

For various reasons, then, there seems to be little point in drawing up comprehensive and allegedly universal schemes for the analysis of illocutionary force based on the existence of a particular set of performative verbs in particular languages. There is perhaps even less point in trying to establish a watertight classification of all possible speech acts in terms of the necessary and sufficient conditions that they must satisfy in order for them to count as instances of one class rather than another. Most speech acts, as I have said, are culture-specific in that they depend upon the legal, religious or ethical conventions and practices institutionalized in particular societies. If the society is one, like our own, with firmly established principles for deciding at law whether something is or is not, let us say, a breach of contract, it may be relatively easy to propose necessary and sufficient conditions constitutive of speech acts of this particular kind. But we are deluding ourselves if we think that all speech acts are regulated, in this way, in the societies in which they operate. Even the act of promising, which looks as if it might be readily definable in terms of the conditions that regulate it, turns out to be problematical from this point of view. It certainly cannot be assumed without argument that promising, in the sense in which we understand the word 'promise', is something that can be done in all languages and in all cultures. And yet assumptions of this kind are commonly made in some of the more specialized work in the theory of speech acts.

Although most speech acts are culture-specific, there are others that are widely, and perhaps correctly, assumed to be universal. They include making *statements*, asking *questions* and issuing *commands*. It has been argued, on philosophical grounds, that these three classes of illocutionary acts are not only universal, but basic – in two senses of 'basic': first, that no human society could exist in which acts of this kind have no role to play; second, that many, if not all, culture-specific illocutionary acts can be seen as belonging to a more specialized subclass of one of the three basic classes. For example, as I mentioned earlier, swearing on oath that something is so is obviously a culture-specific act. But swearing that something is so is also one way of making a strong statement; and statement-making, it is argued, is basic and universal.

I will not go into the question of the relation between basic and non-basic speech acts. However, I would emphasize one point: even if the allegedly basic acts of making statements, asking questions and issuing commands are universal, they too are regulated, in all societies, by more or less culture-specific institutions, practices and beliefs. One recognizable dimension of cultural variation, in this respect, is that of politeness. It is impolite, in all societies, to speak out of turn: that is, to speak when the social role that one is playing does not grant authority and precedence or, alternatively, when the rules that govern turn-taking in that society do not grant one the authority to speak at that point. It is also impolite, in some societies, to be too assertive in the exercise of one's locutionary and illocutionary authority. For example, it might be considered impolite, in certain circumstances, to make a straightforward unqualified assertion or to issue a blunt and unqualified command. The origin and more or less conventionalized use of various kinds of *indirect speech acts* can be explained in such terms as these, as, for example, in English where *Could you pass the sugar?* (originating as a question and commonly so punctuated in its written form) is used in preference to *Pass the sugar* (a direct command).

Politeness, however, is but one of the dimensions of cultural variation that regulate the use of the allegedly basic speech acts. Furthermore, though it has a certain cross-cultural validity and under a sufficiently general interpretation of 'politeness' may be universal, it does not manifest itself in the same way in all societies. One must be careful, therefore, not to assume that generalizations made on the basis of one's experience of one kind of society will be valid in respect of all human societies. I will not develop this point any further. But I would ask the reader to bear it in mind in all that follows. For the discussion and exemplification of the part played by politeness and other factors in the regulation of language-behaviour in different cultures reference may be made to recent work in *sociolinguistics* and *pragmatics*.

Statements, questions and commands

We are assuming that all languages provide their users with the means of making statements, asking questions and issuing commands. It does not follow from this assumption, however, that all languages will grammaticalize these differences of illocutionary force. As we saw in Chapter 6, it is quite possible for sentences to exist that are neutral in sentence-type or mood: sentences that are neither declarative nor interrogative, on the one hand, and are not indicative, subjunctive or imperative, on the other.

Nevertheless, it may well be clear enough what illocutionary act is being performed when one of these sentences is uttered. This may be clear not only from the context in which it occurs, but also from the prosodic structure that is superimposed upon the resultant utterance-inscription. For example, if English had no interrogative sentences, so that

'The door is open'

was not declarative, but neutral in sentence-type, it would be possible to utter this sentence (as *The door is open*) with, let us say, falling intonation to make a statement and rising intonation to ask a question. This point was made earlier. It may now be generalized in terms of the more sophisticated account of the process of uttering sentences that has been outlined in this chapter.

But it was also asserted earlier that many languages, including English, do in fact grammaticalize distinctions of sentence-type and mood: and furthermore that there is an essential connection between sentence-type and mood, on the one hand, and what we are now calling illocution-ary force, on the other. What is the nature of this connection? And how do statements, questions and com-mands differ from one another semantically? I will do no more than provide a partial answer from a particular point of view.

To make a statement is to express a proposition and simultaneously to express a particular attitude towards it. I will call this attitude, for reasons which will be clearer when we look at the notion of modality, *epistemic com-mitment*. (The term 'epistemic', which comes from a Greek word meaning 'knowledge', is used by logicians to refer to the branch of modal logic that deals with knowl-edge and related matters.) Anyone who states a certain proposition is committed to it, not in the sense that he must in fact know or believe it to be true, but in the sense that his subsequent statements – and anything that can be legitimately inferred from his concomitant and subse-quent behaviour – must be consistent with the belief that it is true. Hence the unacceptability of

It is raining but I don't believe it

(construed as a statement). In making any such statement the speaker is guilty of a breach of epistemic commitment.

When one asks a question, one expresses a proposition and simultaneously expresses one's attitude of non-commitment with respect to its truth-value. But there is more to it than this. As was noted in Chapter 6, *Is the door open? – that is a question I refuse to ask* is a perfectly acceptable utterance. In this case a question is posed, but not asked. To ask a question then is not merely to express the propositional attitude of non-commitment – that is, to pose the proposition as a question – but also, in doing so, to indicate to one's interlocutor – prosodically, paralin-guistically or otherwise – that one desires him to resolve one's uncertainty by assigning a truth-value to the prop-osition in question. It follows, for this and other reasons, that questions are not, of their nature, a subclass of commands or requests. They can be posed without being asked; and they do not of themselves require or invite a response.

What then of commands and requests? They differ from statements and factual questions in that they involve a different kind of commitment on the part of the speaker: *deontic commitment*. (The term 'deontic' comes from a Greek word relating to the imposition of obligations. Like 'epistemic', it is borrowed from modal logic.) In issuing a command the speaker commits himself not to the truth, or factuality, of some proposition, but to the necessity of some course of action. To make the same point in more traditional terms: he expresses, not his belief that something is so, but his will that something be so.

In making a request, the speaker also expresses his will that something should be so, but he explicitly concedes to the addressee the right of non-compliance. Requests are in this respect like so-called conducive questions – questions such as

   The door is open, isn't it?,

in the utterance of which the speaker expresses his own commitment to the truth-value of the proposition "The door is open", but simultaneously concedes to the addressee the right to reject it. Another way of making the point is to say that in conducive questions and requests the speaker expresses his commitment to the "it-is-so" or "so-be-it" component of the utterance and invites the addressee to do the same.

The analysis of statements, questions, commands and requests that has been presented in outline here suggests that their illocutionary force can be factorized, in each case, into two components: a component of commitment ("I say so") or non-commitment, on the one hand, and what might be referred to as a *modal* component of factuality ("It is so") *vs* desirability ("so be it"), on the other. I have used the term 'modal' in this connection (instead of introducing some more specialized terminology) for two reasons. First, the distinction between factuality and various kinds of non-factuality falls within the scope of what the logician refers to as modality: I have prepared the way for our treatment of modality by deliberately introducing the terms 'epistemic' and 'deontic'. Second, such distinctions are commonly grammaticalized in languages in the category of *mood*. It is important to realize, however, that mood in natural languages may also grammaticalize different kinds of degrees of commitment. The grammatical category of mood must not be confused with what some logicians refer to as the mood of a proposition. As we shall see later, the logician's formalization of modality and mood rests upon the objectification of the essentially subjective component of commitment.

If a language has a grammatical mood which is used distinctively and characteristically for the purpose of expressing the speaker's unqualified epistemic commitment, that mood is traditionally described as the *indicative*. Similarly, if a language has a grammatical mood which is used distinctively and characteristically for the purpose of imposing one's will on others, that mood is traditionally described as the *imperative*. As we shall see in Chapter 10, there are various ways in which the speaker can qualify his epistemic or deontic commitment. All natural spoken languages provide their users with the prosodic and paralinguistic resources which enable them to do this. Some, but by no means all, grammaticalize different kinds and different degrees of commitment in the category of mood; and some languages lexicalize or semi-lexicalize them by means of modal adverbs and particles.

All this will be taken up later in connection with the notion of subjectivity. I have mentioned it here, without detailed development or exemplification, in order to show how a fairly traditional view of mood can be reformulated within the framework of speech-act theory. As we have seen in this chapter, Austin began by identifying explicit performatives as a rather special class of utterances, in the production of which the speaker is doing something, rather than saying something, by mean of language. He later came to realize that all saying is doing and that all kinds of saying – including the production of statements, questions, commands and requests – are regulated by the central concepts of authority and commitment.

Austin himself emphasized the social basis of these concepts; and at this point he makes contact, though not explicitly, on the one hand with Wittgenstein and, on the other, as we shall see in the next chapter, with Grice. He might just as well have emphasized the personal, or expressive, character of the concepts of authority and commitment. This is what is done in traditional accounts of mood, couched in terms of the speaker's judgment and will. Here, as elsewhere, not only in the use of language, but in all communicative behaviour, the expressive merges with the social and is ultimately indistinguishable from it.

One final point must now be made. The theory of speech acts is sometimes advocated, or criticized, as if it were an alternative to truth-conditional semantics. It should be clear from earlier chapters of this book that the two theories are, in principle, complementary. Truth-conditional semantics is a theory of the propositional content of sentences; speech-act theory – if we grant that it is or aspires to be a theory – deals with the illocutionary force of utterances. Much ink has been spilled recently by linguists and philosophers on the question whether Austin was right or wrong when he said that utterances like *I promise to pay you £5*, when used to make a promise, are neither true nor false, but either efficacious or not. I have said nothing about this controversy here, because in my view it is of no consequence whether we resolve the issue one way or the other. For the illocutionary force of ordinary descriptive statements, like *It is raining*, cannot be accounted for satisfactorily within the framework of truth-conditional semantics. Austin is at one with Frege in making this point. To my mind it is incontrovertible.

Summary

In this chapter, I have dealt in some detail with Austin's theory of speech acts and have shown how it can be used to establish a distinction between sentence-meaning and utterance-meaning. I have paid more attention than either philosophers or linguists usually do to the analysis of locutionary, as distinct from illocutionary, acts: in particular, I have demonstrated that sentences cannot be regarded as classes of utterance-inscriptions. In my treatment of illocutionary force and so-called indirect speech acts, I have emphasized (as Austin did) the sociocultural determinants of meaning. I have also introduced the notions of epistemic and deontic commitment, which will be of central importance in the final chapter of this book.

9. *Understanding Utterances*

Text and context

'The basic assumption . . . is that any text can be regarded as a constituent of a context of situation.'

J.R. Firth, 'Synopsis of linguistic theory'

We have been operating with the assumption that utterance-meaning is crucially dependent on context. So far, however, I have made no attempt to say what context is or how it determines the meaning of utterances and controls our understanding of them. Nor have I said anything about spoken and written text. And yet it is clear that even sentence-sized utterances, of the kind that we considered in the previous chapter, are interpreted on the basis of a good deal of contextual information, most of which is implicit.

In this chapter, I shall be dealing with both text and context. As we shall see, they are complementary: each presupposes the other. Texts are constituents of the contexts in which they are produced; and contexts are created, and continually transformed and refashioned, by the texts that speakers and writers produce in particular situations.

Text-sentences

Before we can talk sensibly about the relation between text and context, we must look again at the status of sentences.

It was pointed out, in the previous chapter, that most of

our everyday utterance-inscriptions are not sentences. Some of them are ready-made locutions of fixed form: *Good Heavens!*, *Least said, soonest mended*, etc. I shall have no more to say about these. I mention them merely to indicate that, in all languages, there are such locutions, finite in number and in some cases of more or less determinate grammatical structure, whose form and meaning cannot be accounted for, synchronically, in terms of the utterance of sentences. They must of course be accounted for in the description of the grammatical and semantic structure of particular languages. But they do not raise problems different in kind from those which arise in the analysis of the infinite set of utterance-inscriptions that result from the utterance of sentences. It is this infinite set of utterance-inscriptions with which we are mainly concerned here. Paradoxical though it may appear, the product of the utterance of a sentence is not necessarily a sentence.

The apparent paradox disappears immediately if we draw a distinction between a more abstract and a more concrete sense of the term 'sentence'. Sentences in the more abstract sense are theoretical constructs, which are postulated by the linguist, in order to account for the acknowledged grammaticality of certain potential utterances and the ungrammaticality of others. They may or may not have some kind of psychological validity in the production and interpretation of language-utterances. But they certainly do not occur as the inscribed, and transcribable, products of utterances. I will refer to sentences in this more abstract sense of the term as *system-sentences*: they are generated by the grammatical rules of some *language-system* (operating upon a vocabulary which belongs to the same language-system).

Let us now introduce the term *text-sentence* for the more concrete sense of 'sentence' – the sense in which sentences are a subclass of utterance-inscriptions and, as such, may occur (in some languages at least) as whole texts or as segments of text. This allows us to say that the

utterance of a particular system-sentence, such as
    'I have not seen Mary',
will result, in some contexts, in the production of a
text-sentence, such as
    I have not seen Mary
(with or without the contraction of *have not* to *haven't*,
and with some contextually appropriate prosodic structure). This may look like the multiplication of theoretical
entities beyond necessity. But there is a very considerable
pay-off.

I have said that the utterance of a sentence is not
necessarily a sentence. This is readily illustrated with
reference to the utterance of 'I have not seen Mary'. Let
us suppose that we are faced with the following text,
either written or spoken:
    Have you seen Mary? I haven't. Peter hasn't either.
    She is never here when should be.
It is composed of four text-units, only the first of which
would normally be described as a complete sentence. All
the others, including *I haven't*, are elliptical sentence-
fragments. And yet, in this context, *I haven't* is just as
much the product of the utterance of 'I have not seen
Mary' as is the text-sentence *I have not seen Mary* in other
contexts. And its propositional content cannot be identified unless we are able to identify the sentence that has
been uttered in the performance of the locutionary act of
which *I haven't*, in this context, is the product. The same
goes, of course, for *Peter hasn't either* with respect to
'Peter has not seen Mary', and for *She is never here when
she should be* with respect to 'Mary is never here when she
should be here'.

It is important to realize that, although I have introduced a certain amount of technical terminology to handle the requisite theoretical distinctions, the distinctions
themselves are real enough in our everyday experience of
the use of language. We have no difficulty in deciding that
I haven't has the propositional content of 'I have not seen
Mary' in one context, of 'I have not been to Switzerland'

in another, of 'I have not got any money' in yet a third, and so on. In fact, out of context *I haven't* is infinitely ambiguous. In context, *I haven't* loses its ambiguity insofar as it is possible to say which of the infinitely many sentences of English with the appropriate grammatical structure has been uttered. I will continue to use the term 'sentence' in both senses, relying upon the notational distinction between single quotation-marks and italics to make it clear what kind of units I am referring to.

What is text?

Text and context, let us agree, are complementary. I will come to context presently. But what is text? One answer that is often given is that a text is a sequence of sentences. As it stands, this is clearly unsatisfactory – if 'sentence' means, as it must in this context, "text-sentence". True, there are some texts that would satisfy the definition, notably texts of a more formal character. But the vast majority of everyday colloquial texts are made up of a mixture of sentences, sentence-fragments and ready-made locutions. However, this defect in the definition of 'text' that has just been given is only one aspect of a more serious deficiency: its failure to make explicit the fact that the units of which a text is composed, whether they are sentences or not, are not simply strung together in sequence, but must be connected in some contextually appropriate way. The text as a whole must exhibit the related, but distinguishable, properties of *cohesion* and *coherence*.

We cannot go into the distinction between cohesion and coherence, as it has been drawn recently by those working in the field of text linguistics and discourse analysis. Roughly speaking, it has to do with the difference between form and content; and some such distinction is both intuitively attractive and theoretically justifiable. To return to our sample text: that the product of the utterance

'I have not seen Mary' should have the form *I haven't*, rather than *I have not seen Mary*, is a matter of cohesion. So too is the use of *either* in *Peter hasn't either* and the use of the pronoun 'she', rather than 'Mary' in the first clause of *She is never here when she is wanted*. Cohesion is destroyed if the first three text-units are put in a different order, such as:

> *Peter hasn't either. I haven't. Have you seen Mary?*

It is also destroyed if we replace each of the text-units with the corresponding full text-sentence.

> *Have you seen Mary? I haven't seen Mary. Peter hasn't seen Mary (either). Mary is never here when she should be here.*

It is evident that this sequence of units does not have the same kind of connectedness that the original sequence of units did. For this reason it is less easy, though not impossible, to take the sequence as text, rather than as a string of unconnected utterances. Ellipsis and the use of pronouns, as well as the use of particular connecting particles and conjunctions (*therefore, so*, etc.) commonly serve to create and sustain that kind of connectedness to which the term 'cohesion' is applied. Languages differ considerably with respect to the degree to which they permit or oblige their users to connect text-units in sequence by means of explicit indications of cohesion.

The other kind of connectedness – coherence – is a matter of content, rather than form. In default of any contextual indication to the contrary, what is being said in any one text-unit is assumed to be *relevant* to what has just been said in the immediately preceding text-units. For example, in our sample text the propositional content of the fourth text-unit *She is never here when she should be* will normally be taken to be relevant to that of the preceding three. In particular, 'she' will be understood to refer to Mary (by virtue of cohesion) and the general statement that the speaker is making about Mary will be understood as a comment upon her absence at that time, rather than as the expression of some totally unconnected

passing thought. Similarly, if we heard or read the following sequence of two text-sentences,

> *The whole family went to town last Saturday.*
> *Veronica bought a dress, while John kept the chil-*
> *dren occupied in the toy-shop,*

we would normally assume that Veronica was one of the
family, and presumably the mother; that she bought the
dress in town; and that the toy-shop was also in town.
None of these propositions has been explicitly formulated, still less asserted; and any one of them might be
contradicted, in specific contexts of utterance, by other
propositions that are part of the speaker's and hearer's
background knowledge.

We shall return to the question of coherence and
relevance later in the chapter. Meanwhile, I would
emphasize three points. First, the question "What is
text?" is far more general then "What is a text?". Texts,
whether written or spoken, are deliberately composed by
their authors as discrete wholes with determinate begin-
nings and endings. Most of the text that we produce in our
day-to-day use of language is not organized in this way
into self-contained texts.

The second point to be noted is that, as I am using the
term 'text', individual text-sentences, sentence-fragments
and fixed locutions all count as text in relation to their
context of utterance, regardless of whether they are
embedded in larger stretches of text or not.

Finally, it must be emphasized that the account that I
gave of speech acts in the previous chapter is intended to
cover, in principle, all aspects of the production of text.
Speech-act theorists have been little concerned, so far,
with anything other than the production of text-sentences.
But the utterance of a sentence, in practice, always
involves its contextualisation: the process of making the
product of utterance both cohesive and coherent in relation to its context. As I have said, text and context are
complementary, What then is context? And how does it
relate to utterance-meaning?

Utterance-meaning and context

Context determines utterance-meaning at three distinguishable levels in the analysis of text. First, it may tell us what sentence has been uttered – if a sentence has indeed been uttered. Second, it will usually tell us what proposition has been expressed – if a proposition has been expressed. Third, it may serve to tell us that the proposition in question has been expressed with one kind of illocutionary force rather than another. In all three respects, context is relevant to the determination of what is said, in the several senses of 'say' that were identified in the preceding chapter.

But utterance-meaning goes beyond what is actually said: it also includes what is implied (or presupposed). And context is highly relevant to this part of the meaning of utterances. In this section, we shall restrict our attention to what is said: to the locutionary and illocutionary aspects of utterance-meaning. We shall rely initially upon an intuitive everyday notion of what context is. That context may tell us what sentence has been uttered is obvious from our discussion of locutionary acts. As we saw, tokens of the same utterance-inscription can result from the utterance, on different occasions, of different sentences. In such cases, the utterance-inscription itself will usually be either grammatically or lexically ambiguous. For example,

> *They passed the port at midnight*

is lexically (and perhaps also grammatically) ambiguous. However, it would normally be clear in context which of the two homonyms, 'port$_1$' ("harbour") or 'port$_2$' ("kind of fortified wine") is being used – and also which sense of the polysemous verb 'pass' is intended. Although polysemy, unlike homonymy, does not give us grounds for distinguishing one sentence from another, it may have the consequence that one sentence has several relatively distinct senses. In collocation with 'port$_2$' the most salient sense of 'pass', out of context, is undoubtedly the one in which it means "hand from one to another". But it is easy to see that in the appropriate context 'pass' meaning "go around" can be collocated with 'port$_2$' just as readily as it can be collocated, in other contexts, with 'port$_1$'.

We do not know what propositional content is being expressed unless we know what sentence is being uttered. Moreover, if the sentence contains one or more polysemous expressions, we do not know in what sense they are being used. Context, therefore, is a factor in the determination of the propositional content of particular tokens of utterance-inscriptions on different occasions of utterance.

Usually, we operate with contextual information below the level of consciousness in our interpretation of every-day utterances. Most of the ambiguities, whether lexical or grammatical, therefore pass unnoticed. For example, 'the vintage port' would be interpreted as referring to wine, and 'the busy port' as referring to a harbour. From time to time, however, we are made aware of such ambiguities, precisely because our contextual informa-tion differs in content or saliency from that of our interlocutor. We may then either fail to understand what he is saying, hesitating between alternative interpreta-tions, or misunderstand his utterance by taking it in the wrong sense. The second of these two possibilities is often exploited by humourists and comedians, who deliberately set up the context in such a way that their audience will unconsciously assign one interpretation to an utterance-inscription and then, in the so-called punch line, suddenly reveal to them, more or less indirectly, that they have been led up the garden path.

In some cases there is no need to set up the context specially for the purpose. The out-of-context saliency of what is subsequently revealed to be the garden-path interpretation will suffice. To take a rather hackneyed example: if

Three strong girls went for a tramp

is followed, after a brief pause, with
    The tramp died,
the comedian will probably secure the desired effect, simply by virtue of the out-of-context saliency of the sense of 'go for a tramp' in which it falls, semantically and syntactically, with 'go for a walk', 'go for a ride', 'go for a swim', etc.

Both contextually determined and out-of-context saliency are, of course, exploited for more serious purposes in literature, where the reader may well be expected to hold two or more interpretations in mind simultaneously and either hesitate between them or combine them, in some way, to construct a richer composite interpretation. Ambiguity is commonly described by philosophers and linguists as if it were of its nature pathological – something which gets in the way of clarity and precision. This is a highly prejudiced and unbalanced view of the matter. Not only is it frequently, and erroneously, associated with the view that all sentences have precise and determinate meanings; it is based on the equally erroneous assumption that clarity and the avoidance of vagueness and equivocation are always desirable, regardless of what language-game we are playing. Nothing that is said about ambiguity in this section, or anywhere else in this book, should be taken to imply that ambiguity is, or should be, avoided in all contexts.

Let us now turn to the second of the two levels at which context determines utterance-meaning: to the fact that context can tell us what proposition has been expressed. In Part 3, 1 drew a distinction between 'proposition' and 'propositional content', and a corresponding distinction between 'reference' and 'referential range'. I pointed out that, whereas the propositional content of a sentence and the referential range of its constituent expressions can be established without appeal to the context of utterance, it is not generally possible to establish the actual reference of referring expressions, and thus to establish what proposition is being expressed, without knowing in what context a sentence is uttered. We can now relate this point to the immediately preceding discussion of text and context.

As we have seen, *I haven't* can be put into correspondence, by means of the notion of contextualization, with any one of an infinite set of sentences. In our sample text, it can be identified as the product of the utterance of the sentence 'I have not seen Mary', which contains two referring expressions: 'I' and 'Mary'. What do they refer to? Obviously, there is no way of knowing. If we make certain assumptions about the production of the text, we can say that the speaker or writer – more generally, the locutionary agent – is referring to himself by means of 'I' and to some person other than himself and his addressee by means of 'Mary'. It is worth noting, however, that we cannot be sure even of this simply on the basis of our knowledge of English. There are circumstances in which a speaker may refer to someone other than himself by means of 'I', notably when he is acting as a spokesman or interpreter; and there are circumstances in which one may refer to one's addressee by name. In any case, granted that the locutionary agent is referring to himself with 'I' and to someone else with 'Mary' (and that a proposition is being expressed), we cannot say what proposition is being expressed and evaluate it for truth or falsity without knowing who the locutionary agent and Mary are.

We also need to know when the utterance was produced. The fact that the locutionary agent said *haven't*, rather than *didn't, hadn't, don't* (or *can't*), is relevant to the truth-value of the proposition that he expresses. (So too, incidentally, is the fact that in most contexts there will be a tacitly understood reference to the period of time of which the predicative expression 'have seen' is, or is not, true. For example, the speaker may have seen Mary on the previous day, or even a very short time before, and yet be held to have made a true statement in saying *I haven't*.) In the case of other utterances, we need to know, not only the time, but also the place of utterance, in order to establish what proposition has been expressed. For example, this is the case in respect of *She is never here when she should be*: 'here' normally refers to the place of utterance, so that "Mary is here" will be true of one location at certain times and false of that location at other times. Questions of this kind will occupy us in Chapter 10. Let us merely note for the present that the vast majority of utterance-inscriptions in most languages are implicitly, if not explicitly, *indexical* or *deictic*, so that they express different propositions according to the context in which they are produced. This point has already been mentioned in connection with the treatment of sentence-meaning in Montague semantics in Chapter 7.

We come, finally, to the contextual determination of illocutionary force. As we saw in the preceding chapter, the same sentence may by uttered on different occasions with different kinds of illocutionary force. For example,

> 'I will give you £5'

may be uttered as promise or a prediction. Or again,

> 'Sit down'

may be uttered, in what is normally regarded as its most characteristic use, as a request or a command; it may also be used in order to grant the addressee permission to sit down. Frequently, but not always, the prosodic contour will indicate to the addressee that the utterance has one kind of illocutionary force rather than another. But whether this is also indicated prosodically or not (in the case of spoken utterances), it will usually be clear, in context, what kind of illocutionary act has been performed. For example, it will usually be clear whether the speaker has the authority to order the addressee to sit down or to grant him permission to do so.

Indeed, much of our day-to-day language-behaviour is so closely integrated with other kinds of social behaviour that the occurrence of an utterance with a particular illocutionary force is often predictable from the socially identifiable situation in which it is embedded. We would not normally sit down in someone else's house or office without being invited to. On the other hand, in most situations – paying a call on a new neighbour, coming to see the bank-manager about an overdraft, etc., – it will be evident to us and to our interlocutor that at a certain point in the conversation an invitation of this kind should be made. This being so, the addressee does not have to compute the illocutionary force of *Sit down*, from first principles, in terms of the meaning of the sentence 'Sit down' and his assessment of the speaker's motivation for saying what he has said. The situation itself predisposes him to expect either this very utterance-inscription or another with the same illocutionary force (*Won't you sit down?*, *Why don't you take a seat?*, etc). It is arguable that most so-called indirect speech acts, of the kind that were mentioned in the previous chapter, can be accounted for in this way. At any rate, there can be no doubt that the illocutionary force of an utterance is strongly determined by the context in which it occurs.

Context determines utterance-meaning, then, at three distinguishable levels in the analysis of text. I shall make no attempt, for the moment, to say what context is or how it is handled theoretically. From what has been said in this section, however, it will be evident that the context of an utterance includes, not only the surrounding *co-text* (if there is any), but also the relevant features of the situation of utterance. As we shall see later, what is sometimes referred to as the *context of situation* can, and should, be defined in such a way that it subsumes everything in the co-text that bears upon the question of coherence. It is for this reason that I chose a quotation from Firth for the introduction to this chapter.

Implication and implicatures

There is an everyday sense of the verb 'imply' in which we can, and usually do, imply by means of our utterances something other than what we actually say. For example, asked to give an opinion about a person's character, I

might say
> *He'd share his last crust of bread with you.*

Obviously, I have not said of the person in question that he is both kind and generous. But I might reasonably be held to have implied this.

Much of the information that is conveyed from speaker to hearer in day-to-day conversation is implied, rather than asserted. In some cases, of course, it is not clear whether the speaker intends the hearer to draw a particular inference or not. And this opens the way for misunderstanding and misrepresentation, on the one hand, and for the subtle manipulation of the hearer's opinion, on the other. However, in what one may think of as the standard kind of situation, not only does the hearer draw the inferences that the speaker intends him to draw, but they are such that the speaker himself, if asked, would also subscribe to them. I have assumed that this is so in respect of the example in the preceding paragraph. It is easy enough to devise a situation in which the hearer would not draw the inference that the person referred to is kind and generous. It is equally easy to think of circumstances in which the speaker might insincerely and deceitfully intend him to draw this inference.

In recent years, the notion of *implicature* has been introduced into the philosophy of language, and subsequently into linguistics, to bridge some of the gap between the logical notions of implication and entailment, on the one hand, and the broader everyday notion of implication, on the other. According to Grice in his 1967/8 William James lectures (see Grice, 1975), there are two kinds of implicatures: conventional and conversational. The difference between them is that the former depend upon something other than what is truth-conditional in the conventional use, or meaning, of particular forms and expressions, whereas the latter derive from a set of more general principles which regulate the proper conduct of conversation.

It has been argued, for example, that the difference

between *but* and *and* in English can be accounted for in terms of the notion of conventional implicature. Those who take this view, including Grice himself, would say that the following two sentences have the same propositional content:

'She is poor and she is honest',
'She is poor but she is honest'.

If they also identify sentence-meaning with propositional content, they would say that the two sentences have the same meaning. I gave it as my view in Chapter 6 that most people would probably disagree. The proponents of truth-conditional semantics can meet this challenge – if they accept that there is such a thing as conventional implicature – by attributing the apparent difference in meaning to the conventional implicature associated with *but*. They can say that the use of *but*, in contrast with *and*, indicates that the speaker feels that there is some kind of contrast between the conjoined propositions.

For example, on the assumption that the two sentences are being used to make an assertion and 'she' refers to the same person in each of the conjoined clauses, in saying

She is poor but she is honest

the speaker might be implicating (though not asserting) that it is unusual for anyone to be both poor and honest. But would the implication, or implicature, be as determinate as this? Out of context there is no way of knowing exactly which of several propositions the speaker is implicating. He might be surprised, not that anyone should be poor and honest, but that a woman should be; or, alternatively, that anyone in this person's circumstances or this person in any circumstances should be. Indeed, the speaker may not be indicating his own surprise at all, but merely his expectation that his interlocutor will be surprised. In fact, there is a whole range of further possibilities, most of which can be subsumed in a general sort of way under the notion of contrast. But it is remarkably difficult, in most cases, to say exactly what is being implicated by the use of *but* and impossible to do so without considering in some detail the actual context of utterance.

It is usually taken for granted by those who have discussed the notion of implicature that the difference between *and* and *but* cannot be part of the propositional content of the compound clauses in which they occur; and I tacitly accepted this view in Chapter 6. But there are circumstances in which a speaker can use *but* and *and* contrastively within the scope of 'say', and even of 'true'. For example, he might claim at some point in argument that his interlocutor is misrepresenting him:

> *I did not say that she was poor but honest. I said that she was poor and honest. And that's a very different thing. Personally, I don't find it surprising that anyone should be both. Let us recapitulate then. It is true that she is poor and honest; it is not true – in my view at least – that she is poor but honest. We both subscribe to the truth of the proposition that she is poor and she is honest. We appear to disagree as to the truth of the proposition that she is poor but she is honest.*

I have deliberately constructed this passage in such a way that it starts with an everyday use of 'say' and ends with what is a recognizably technical use of 'proposition'. There is little doubt, I think, that it is more natural to use *but* and *and* contrastively within the scope of 'say' than within the scope of 'proposition'. And yet the passage, as a whole, is surely acceptable.

It is not difficult to find or to construct similar examples in which compound clauses containing *but* can be used after the verb 'say' in what appears to be, at least, the meaning of 'assert'. This does not prove that *but* contributes something other than what *and* does to the propositional content of such clauses. What it does show, however, is that the distinction between what is said and what is conventionally implicated is not always clear in the everyday use of the verb 'say'. More important, it also shows how the lexical and grammatical resources of a particular language can be exploited to propositionalize what is not of its nature propositional. This point is of the greatest importance. It will be taken up and given further exemplification in the following chapter.

The only other example that Grice himself gives to illustrate his notion of conventional implicature is the use of *therefore*. Once we look at the full range of language-use, however, rather than simply at more or less formal argumentation, as Grice does, we can extend the list of forms which meet his criteria for conventional implicature very considerably. Many of the forms that serve to give cohesion to a text, linking one text-unit with another, fall within the scope of his definition: *however*, *moreover*, *nevertheless*, *and yet*, etc. So too do the so-called modal particles like *even*, *well*, or *just*, as in the following utterances:

> *Even Horace likes caviare*,
> *You may well be right*,
> *It was just one of those things*.

English, like French, has relatively few modal particles, in comparison with German, Russian and many other languages. But it does have some. Furthermore, their meaningfulness and their conventionality is evident from the fact that they can be mistranslated; and it is worth noting that mistranslation is possible even where exact translation is not.

A second point to be made is that there seems to be no reason to restrict the notion of conventional implicature to connectives and particles. As we saw in Part 2, many fully lexical expressions are descriptively synonymous, but differ in respect of their social and expressive meaning. Most, if not all, of this difference would seem to fall within the scope of Grice's definition of conventional implicature. So too does much of the difference that is carried in particular contexts by the choice of one form of an expression, rather than another. For example, if the speaker says

> *Christ tells us to love our neighbour*

or
>   *Christ has told us to love our neighbour*

rather than
>   *Christ told us to love our neighbour*,

he can be held to have implicated that Christ's injunction
or exhortation had, and still retains, a certain authority
and validity. In fact, the choice of tense and mood is
commonly associated with semantic and pragmatic differences of this kind. Even if we restrict ourselves to
the medium-transferable, verbal part of utterance-
inscriptions, we can see that a much broader range of
resources than such forms as *but, therefore, even,* etc. can
be used by speakers to implicate something over and
above what they actually say.

A third, and final, point is that, just as there is no
reason to limit the applicability of the notion of conventional implicature to more or less formal argumentation,
so there is no reason to limit it to propositional, or
descriptive, meaning. I have already suggested that differences of social and expressive meaning among descriptively synonymous expressions (insofar as they are
lexicalized in particular languages) can be brought within
the scope of the notion of conventional implicature. But
social and expressive meaning is conveyed at all levels of
language-structure; and it is very heterogeneous. Few
logicians or linguists would wish to push the notion of conventional implicature as far as I have done. Indeed, there
are many who would deny that it has any validity at all.
Some would argue that the alleged implicatures are either
entailments or are implicatures of the kind that Grice
called conversational, rather than conventional. Others,
who have no prior theoretical commitment to an exclusively truth-conditional definition of 'meaning', would
simply point out that all sorts of meaning are given recognition – that is, in Grice's terms, made conventional – in the
grammatical and lexical structure of particular languages.

Grice's so-called conversational implicatures have
aroused far more attention in linguistics than have his

conventional implicatures. I say "so-called" because the ordinary sense of 'conversational' is much narrower. We are not concerned solely with conversations, but with all kinds of social interaction involving either spoken or written language.

The basic idea is that language-behaviour, most typically, is a form of purposive social interaction governed by the principle of co-operation. In essence, Grice argues that we expect people to behave rationally and co-operatively, and we therefore interpret their utterances as if they were being rational and co-operative.

Grice recognizes several kinds of co-operation which he groups, somewhat whimsically, under the headings of quantity, quality, relation and manner. Each of these comprises a set of one or more sub-principles, formulated by Grice as prescriptive maxims, which participants normally obey, but may on occasion violate.

For example, the two maxims having to do with quantity are: (1) Make your contribution as informative as is required; (2) Do not make your contribution more informative than is required. By appealing to these we can account for the fact that, if X asks

> *Have you done the washing-up and put everything away?*

and Y replies

> *I've done the washing-up*,

Y may be held to have implied, in most contexts, that he has not put everything away. This implication, or implicature, derives from his presumably deliberate failure to say *Yes* or its equivalent to the composite proposition that is put to him. The simple proposition "I have done the washing-up" is less informative than "I have done the washing-up and I have put everything away". On the assumption that Y is being duly co-operative and is being sufficiently informative, X can reasonably infer that Y cannot truthfully assert "I have put everything away".

Similarly, by appealing to the maxim "Be relevant" (classified under the heading of relation), we can impose an interpretation on the following exchange:

> X: *The clock is slow.*
>
> Y: *There was a power cut this morning*.

We assume that the propositional content of Y's statement bears some relation to that of X's, in particular that Y is, or might be, supplying an explanation for what X asserts to be the case. Of course, our assumption that Y's utterance is relevant to X's in this way depends not only upon our background knowledge about electric clocks, but also upon the further assumption that Y shares this background knowledge and knows that the clock in question is, or might be, operated by electricity directly supplied from the mains. It is easy to see that such everyday exchanges as the above may depend for their coherence – for the property of connectedness in virtue of which we classify them readily enough as texts – upon a whole set of assumptions of this kind, specific to particular cultures and to particular groups.

Much of the interest aroused by Grice's work on conversational implicatures derives from its explanatory potential in respect of a variety of phenomena that are troublesome from the viewpoint of formal semantics. They include metaphorical interpretation, indirect speech acts and the assertion of tautologies and contradictions. Limitations of space prevent me from dealing with all of these. It may be helpful, however, to say something about the applicablity of Grice's maxims of co-operative interaction by means of language to the interpretation of metaphors.

I will take as my example the following sentence:

> 'John is a tiger',

which has both a literal and a metaphorical interpretation. Before considering it in the light of Grice's principles of co-operative interaction, I should like to reiterate the point I made about the literal interpretation of such sentences at the end of Chapter 5.

Linguists have often described them as either anomalous or contradictory. However, provided that it does not violate conditions of categorical congruity of such generality that it could not be interpreted in any possible world, a sentence of this kind is perfectly well-formed semantically and the proposition it purports to express is not contradictory. Looked at from this point of view, 'John is a tiger' has a non-contradictory literal interpretation, even if 'John' is being used to refer to a person. Indeed, there are all sorts of everyday situations in which 'John is a tiger' might be uttered (with reference to a man or boy) to assert a true proposition. For instance, John might be playing the role of a tiger in a play about animals. The proposition "John is a tiger" would then be true, under a literal interpretation of 'tiger' (and also, incidentally, of the verb 'be'). I mention this kind of interpretation of the sentence in question in order to show that we may not need to adjust our ontological assumptions to any significant degree in the assignment of a literal interpretation to sentences which, at first sight, might look as if they cannot sustain one.

It is also worth noting that there is no closer connection between literal sense and truth-conditionality than there is between metaphorical sense and truth-conditionality. If a statement is made metaphorically by uttering the sentence 'John is a tiger', the proposition thereby expressed – whichever proposition it is – will have just as determinate a truth-value as a proposition like "John is ferocious" or "John is dynamic". Granted, there may be some indeterminacy attaching to the process of metaphorical interpretation itself: it may not be clear to the addressee which of several metaphorical interpretations he should assign to the utterance. But this is comparable with the problem of deciding which of the several literal senses of a polysemous expression is the one intended; and it has nothing to do with truth-conditionality as such.

I am not saying, of course, that all metaphorical expressions are truth-conditionally determinate, but simply that they do not differ from non-metaphorical expressions in terms of a characteristically distinctive, context-dependent indeterminacy. Many metaphorical statements will certainly be truth-conditionally indeterminate; and many will contain an expressive component, which might be held to affect the determinacy of truth-value. But in this respect they are no different from non-metaphorical statements, like *Mary is beautiful* or indeed *John is ferocious* and *John is dynamic*. Linguists who distinguish semantics from pragmatics by means of the criterion of truth-conditionality and ascribe the metaphorical interpretation of utterances to pragmatics are inclined to get confused about questions like this – especially if they also conflate the semantics/pragmatics distinction with the competence/performance distinction.

How then do Grice's maxims of co-operative interaction apply to the process of metaphorical interpretation? The general answer is not that they guide the addressee in his search for one metaphorical interpretation rather than another, but that they motivate the search itself. Hearing or reading *John is a tiger*, the addressee is supposed to reason as follows, saying to himself as it were:

> *The speaker/writer cannot mean that literally. However, I have no grounds for believing that he is being unco-operative. His utterance has the form of a statement. Therefore, he must be trying to tell me something, which presumably makes sense to us both (in the light of our beliefs and assumptions about the world, etc.). He must also believe (if he is being co-operative) that I can work out the non-literal meaning for myself – presumably on the basis of the literal meaning (of the whole utterance-inscription or of one or more of its constituent expressions). One contextually acceptable way of using language to convey something other than what is actually said is by means of metaphor. Let me see whether I can interpret the utterance metaphorically.*

I have spelt this out in some detail (though I have omitted one or two steps in the reasoning) in order to emphasize the multiplicity of assumptions that go into Gricean explanations of metaphor and other phenomena.

Let me now make explicit a few of the points that are implicit in the above account of the addressee's reasoning. First, his assumption or inference that the utterance-inscription cannot have a literal interpretation does not depend upon its being semantically anomalous or contradictory: all that is required is that the literal sense should be contextually improbable. Second, the whole process is subject to the constraints imposed by the participants' beliefs and assumptions (including their beliefs and assumptions about one another's beliefs and assumptions): all communication is subject to such constraints. Third, I have included as a separate step the addressee's recognition of the contextual appropriateness of metaphor: in certain contexts metaphor is more frequently used than in others. Indeed, there may well be occasions, determined by the socio-cultural situation or literary genre, when the use of metaphor is so common that the addressee can skip the earlier steps in the reasoning process outlined above the start with the assumption that a statement is more likely to be meant metaphorically than literally.

As I have said, Grice's notion of conversational implicature gives us no assistance at all when it comes to the problem of deciding upon one metaphorical interpretation of 'John is a tiger' rather than another. But that is not its purpose. Grice's aim was to maintain, as strictly and as consistently as possible, the distinction between what is actually said and what is conveyed (over and above or instead of what is said) by the fact of saying it (and not saying something else).

The explanatory potential of Grice's maxims is, in principle, very considerable. So far, however, the maxims themselves have been applied at a fairly intuitive level. Attempts have been made to formalize them within a predictive theory of the interpretation of texts. But no such attempt has yet won general acceptance. Most treatments rely on a purely impressionistic notion of what constitutes quantity of information, relevance, brevity and orderliness.

What is context?

One of the points that emerges from our discussion of Grice's notion of conversational implicature in the previous section is the double role played by context. First of all, the utterance itself is embedded in what J.R. Firth and others have called a context of situation; and, as we saw in our discussion of metaphor, it may be of importance in deciding whether a metaphorical interpretation is probable or not, to know what the context of situation is. Second, having decided that something is being conveyed over and above what has been said, the addressee has to infer what this is on the basis of contextual information shared by him and his interlocutor.

There has been a tendency, until recently, for linguists and philosophers to neglect the context of situation in their presentation of Grice's maxims. It is arguable that they have, for this reason, failed to bring out as clearly as they should have done the fact that language-behaviour is a culture-dependent activity. What constitutes sincerity and politeness may differ considerably from one society to another. Nor can we assume that rationality will manifest itself, in relation to the quality of information or its relevance, in the same way in all cultures. In fact, Grice's own presentation, and that of many of his followers, may well suffer from some degree of socio-cultural bias – a bias which is now being corrected by those working in conversational analysis and what has come to be called the ethnography of speaking.

It is arguable that Grice's work also suffers from its philosophical bias in favour of descriptive, or propositional, meaning. This is revealed, not only in his acceptance of a truth-conditional theory of meaning, but also in his conception of context – in the second of its two roles referred to above. For him, and for many of those who have drawn upon his ideas, context is taken to be a set of propositions in relation to which new propositions can be evaluated for truth and added to the context (or rejected as untrue).

But much of the knowledge that is involved in the production and interpretation of utterance-inscriptions is practical, rather than propositional: it is a matter of knowing how to do something, not of knowing that something is the case. Of course, it is always possible (in certain languages at least) to describe practical knowledge as if it were propositional. For example, instead of saying that a speaker must be able to tell whether his interlocutor is of higher or lower social status, we can say that the speaker must know which, if either, of the following two propositions is true: "X is of higher status than Y" and "X is of lower status than Y" (where X and Y stand for referring expressions which will identify the speaker and addressee respectively). However, the fact that we can formulate practical knowledge in propositional terms does not mean that it is in fact propositional. A strong case can be made for the view (taken for granted throughout this work) that social and expressive information is non-propositional.

It would seem, therefore, that context in both of the roles identified earlier in this section is, to a considerable degree, non-propositional. One of the advantages of the theory of speech acts that we looked at in the previous chapter is that, in Austin's formulation at least, it gives full recognition to the social basis of language. It is, as I said, a theory of social pragmatics (in the etymological sense of 'pragmatics'): a theory of a particular kind of social doing. Grice's notion of language-behaviour as co-operative interaction fits in well with this; and, as I mentioned at the end of the preceding section, it need not be coupled with the assumption that the norms, or maxims, that he has formulated for one kind of discourse in one culture – one kind of language-game, as Wittgenstein would have put it – are universally valid.

No simple answer, then, can be given to the question "what is context?". I have discussed it in some detail elsewhere, and others have done so too, with extensive exemplification. Here I shall be content to emphasize the fact that, in the construction of a satisfactory theory of context, the linguist's account of the interpretation of utterances must of necessity draw upon, and will in turn contribute to, the theories and findings of the social sciences in general: notably of psychology, anthropology and sociology.

Summary

In this chapter, I have demonstrated the interdependence of text and context, and I have shown how context is relevant to the interpretation of utterances on several different levels. Grice's notions of conventional and conversational implicatures have been explained, in general and with particular reference to metaphor. Finally, I have emphasized the importance of distinguishing between the propositional and the non-propositional parts of a context, and of handling the latter within the framework of a general theory of what might be appropriately described as social pragmatics.

10 *Worlds within Worlds*

The subjectivity of utterance

'There are more things in heaven and earth, Horatio,
Than are dreamt of in your philosophy.'
William Shakespeare, *Hamlet*

Having looked at the notion of context in some detail in
the preceding chapter, we can now return to the question
of speech acts and locutionary agency. We shall begin
with *reference* – the relation that holds between linguistic
expressions and what they stand for in the world, or
universe of discourse. We shall then take up a particular
kind of reference, *deixis*, which depends crucially upon
the time and place of utterance and upon the speaker's
and addressee's roles in the utterance-act itself. This will
lead us into a discussion of *modality* and other characteristically subjective aspects of locutionary agency.

Reference

Reference, as we have seen at various points in this book,
is a context-dependent aspect of utterance-meaning: it is a
relation that holds between speakers (more generally,
locutionary agents) and what they are talking about on
particular occasions. The *referential range* of referring
expressions is fixed by their meaning in the language (i.e.,
by their sense and denotation). But their actual reference
depends upon a variety of contextual factors.

We cannot generally determine the reference of an
expression, then, without regard to its context of utterance. What we can do, within the restrictions of sentence-
based semantics, is to establish the *intension* of the

expression. As we saw in Chapter 7, model-theoretic semantics (of which Montague's system is a particular version) does in fact incorporate reference within sentence-meaning – by making the meaning of a sentence relative to an *index* (or point of reference), in which all the relevant contextual information is specified. But this does not affect the substance of what has been said here about reference as a part of utterance-meaning. Model-theoretic semantics operates with a different notion of sentence-meaning; and, as we saw in Chapter 7, it adopts a particular definition of 'intension'. We shall not be concerned with these differences of definition and formalization in the present chapter. But we shall take up, at an intuitive and informal level, the notions of possible worlds and intensionality, which were introduced in Part 3 in connection with Montague grammar.

Simple propositions are normally analysed by logicians into expressions of two kinds: names and predicates. Names serve to pick out – to *refer* to – entities (or sets of entities) in some possible world about which statements are being made; predicates serve to ascribe properties to single entities (or single sets) and relations to ordered pairs, triples, etc. of entities (or sets). All this is formalized in standard predicate logic.

Names, in the everyday sense of the word 'name', are not the only kind of referring expressions. Also, they are from a semantic point of view rather special in that, of themselves and in languages like English, they have no descriptive content. (The qualification "in languages like English" is intended to indicate that natural languages may vary with respect to the way naming operates and is integrated with other cultural practices and customs. Philosophical discussions of proper names rarely mention this possibility or its theoretical significance.) For example, 'Napoleon' is arbitrarily associated with indefinitely many entities (persons, animals, ships, etc.) which in principle have nothing in common. True, one of these entities – or some concept, or intension, associated with him – is salient, in the culture in which English is commonly used, by virtue of his historical importance. (And some of the others have acquired their names as a consequence of this fact and of its actual or attributed significance in the light of the conventions that regulate the assignment of names in particular cultures.) This means that, in default of specific contextual information to the contrary, for most speakers of English the name 'Napoleon' will usually be taken to refer to this culturally salient entity. It also means that there will be a whole host of shared associations and connotations clustering around the name 'Napoleon', which go to make up what some philosophers refer to as the intension, or individual concept, "Napoleon". However, it does not mean that the name 'Napoleon' as such has any descriptive content or sense.

Apart from proper names, there are two main subclasses of referring expressions that are distinguishable, both syntactically and semantically, in English: noun-headed noun-phrases and pronouns. Actually, the traditional analysis of what I am calling *noun-headed noun-phrases* (e.g., 'the boy', 'those four old houses') can be challenged on both syntactic and semantic grounds. For simplicity, I will adopt the conventional view, according to which it is indeed the noun that is the head, or principal constituent, in such phrases: hence my term 'noun-headed'. It is also worth pointing out that I am here (and elsewhere in this book) using the term 'noun-phrase' in the sense that it has acquired recently in linguistics. Noun-phrases, in this sense, are not necessarily composed of more than one word.

In some languages, words denoting classes of entities can be employed without any accompanying modifier (definite or indefinite article, demonstrative adjective, etc.) to refer to individual entities: this is not the case in English, where nouns like 'man' or 'tree' cannot be employed, without modification by means of a determiner ('the', 'that', etc.), a quantifier ('one', etc.) or some more complex expression, to refer to individuals. But languages vary considerably in this respect, and there are many differences of detail among languages which fall into one class (English, French, German, etc.) and languages which fall into another (Russian, Latin, etc.). I mention this fact because most of the discussion of referring expressions in general, and of noun-headed noun-phrases in particular, in the recent literature is skewed towards languages that behave, syntactically, more or less like English. My treatment of reference in this book is highly selective and, of necessity, uses examples from English. I must, therefore, emphasize the importance of bearing constantly in mind the fact that English is only one of several thousand natural languages, many of which do things differently.

Noun-headed noun-phrases can be classified semantically in several ways. One subclass to which philosophers have devoted considerable attention is that of *definite descriptions*: expressions which refer to some definite entity and identify it, in part, by means of the descriptive content of the expression. English examples include 'the man' and 'John's father'. As the term 'definite description' suggests, all such expressions may be factorized, semantically if not always syntactically and lexically, into two components. One of these, as we have just noted, is descriptive (e.g., the word 'man' in 'the man'); the other is purely referential (e.g., the definite article, 'the', in English). I shall come back to this purely referential component of definite descriptions in the following section. Here it will suffice to point out that it is non-descriptive, in that it does not identify the entity that is being referred to by means of any of its context-independent properties.

The head-noun (e.g., 'man' in 'the man') will be more or less descriptive of the referent according to the specificity or generality of its sense. At the limit of generality in English is the word 'entity', which can be used to refer to physical and non-physical objects and was deliberately created by philosophers to have exactly the degree of generality that it does have. Since it is descriptively unrestricted, it can combine freely with any other modifying adjective, noun, relative clause, prepositional phrase, etc. But the vast majority of entity-denoting nouns in English are not like this. They fall into different *sortal categories* according to what are held to be the essential (or ontologically necessary) properties of the classes of entities that they denote. Similarly for verbs, adjectives, adverbs, etc.: they too fall into more or less general categories according to the generality or specificity of their sense. (This is the source of what I have called categorial incongruity and have distinguished from contradiction: see Chapter 7.)

The two logically separable components of definite descriptions give rise to two different kinds of presupposition: existential and sortal (or categorial). For example, if one uses the expression 'the man', in what I will call an ordinary context, one is committed to the presupposition that the referent exists and that it is of a particular sort, or category. It is existential presupposition, however, that has been most extensively discussed in recent years by both philosophers and linguists. The reason is that the violation of an existential presupposition, unlike the violation of a sortal presupposition (e.g., *Quadruplicity drinks procrastination, Thursday is in bed with Friday:* see Chapter 5) cannot be accounted for as being in any way anomalous within the framework of sentence-based semantics. To take the now famous example: there is nothing wrong with the sentence

'The present King of France is bald'.

It is in the utterance of this sentence at a time when there is no King of France that the existential presupposition is violated.

I will not go into the various controversies associated with the notion of existential presupposition. I will simply point out that, on the view of sentences, utterances and propositions taken in this book, anyone who deliberately violates an existential presupposition in using what purports to be a definite description fails to express any proposition at all. Looked at in this way, much of the recent discussion of presupposition – important though it may appear to those who are committed to a strictly truth-conditional theory of meaning – seems to be little short of vacuous.

But there are important things to be said in this connection. First, it is not just definite descriptions that involve existential presuppositions, but referring expressions of all kinds. Reference is intrinsically connected with existence; one cannot refer to something that does not exist. One can, of course, refer to fictional and hypothetical entities; but in doing so, one presupposes that they exist in a fictional or hypothetical world.

Second, the falsity of the descriptive content of a referring expression – whether it is a definite description or not – does not nullify the act of reference and render it void. One can successfully, but mistakenly, refer to someone or something by means of a description which, as it happens, is false. Let us suppose, for example, that X and Y are at a cocktail party and that X notices some third person, Z, holding in his hand a tumbler filled with a colourless liquid and also containing ice and lemon. In these circumstances X might successfully refer to Z for the benefit of Y by using the expression 'the man (over there) drinking gin and tonic'. We shall come back to the meaning of the bracketed 'over there' in the next section: here it is sufficient to note that, whether an expression of this kind is added to the definite description or not, in the circumstances that I have envisaged there will commonly be some gesture or other signal drawing the addressee's attention to the referent. Let us now further suppose that Z's glass contains, not gin and tonic, but water – and even that Z is not drinking it, or anything else, but merely holding it for someone else. The fact that the descriptive content of the 'the man drinking a gin and tonic' is false does not mean that *X* has failed to refer to *Z*. Indeed, *X* need not be mistaken about the facts. There are all sorts of everyday situations in which, out of politeness or for other reasons, we refer to people, animals or things by means of descriptions that we know or believe to be false (*Where did you get that beautiful dress?*, etc.).

I will not pursue this matter. What I want to emphasize is that definite descriptions – more obviously than proper names – are context-dependent. Their use as referring expressions cannot be satisfactorily accounted for solely within the framework of sentence-based truth-conditional semantics. When a speaker employs a definite description, he indicates by means of the referential part of the expression that he is performing the act of reference, and tacitly assures the addressee that the descriptive part of the expression will contain all the information that is required, in context, to identify the referent. Various qualifications and elaborations would need to be added in a fuller treatment. But this is the central point.

Definite descriptions are only one of many subclasses of noun-headed noun-phrases used as referring expressions. Another, of course, is that of indefinite descriptions (in certain contexts and used with what is called specific, though not definite, reference): 'a man', 'a certain girl', etc. A third, which has been the object of a good deal of discussion and research, is that of so-called quantified noun-phrases: 'all men', 'every girl', etc. All sorts of previously unsuspected problems have arisen in the attempts that have been made to formalize the notion of reference and put it on a sound theoretical footing. I will mention just one, since it is closely related to the principal concerns of this chapter: the problem of *referential opacity*.

A referentially opaque context is one in which the substitution of one referring expression for another expression with the same reference does not necessarily hold constant the truth conditions of the sentence in which the substitution is made. (I have stated the principle in respect of sentences and truth-conditions. With the necessary adjustments it can also be stated for utterances and truth-values.) I have already illustrated this phenomenon in Chapter 7 (without, however, introducing the term 'opacity'). I pointed out, it will be recalled, that

'I want to meet Margaret Thatcher'

and

'I want to meet the first woman prime minister of Britain'

do not necessarily have the same truth-conditions. This is because 'the first woman prime minister of Britain' can be given either a straightforward extensional interpretation, in which it serves to identify a particular person (in the way that has been outlined in this section) or an intensional interpretation, in which – to make the point rather crudely and perhaps tendentiously for the moment – what counts is not the actual person that the addressee has in mind, but some concept that fits the descriptive content of the expression.

This kind of intensionality is traditionally identified by means of the Latin phrase *de dicto* ("about what is said"), contrasted in this case with *de re* ("about the thing"), which are widely employed nowadays in modal logic and semantics, in the sense indicated here. We shall return to the question of intensionality, in relation to reference, in a later section. Here it is sufficient to note that such generally accepted *de re/de dicto* ambiguities of the kind illustrated here give us particularly cogent reasons for extending the theory of reference beyond the bounds of what I have loosely and inadequately called ordinary contexts. Indeed, it is arguable, as we shall see later, that there is much more intensionality involved in so-called ordinary contexts than is generally supposed. Throughout this section, however, I have been adopting a fairly conventional view of reference.

The third main subclass of referring expressions, in addition to names and noun-headed noun-phrases, is that of pronouns. Much of what has been said here about reference applies also to them. Since they are intrinsically connected with deixis and indexicality, I will deal with them in the next section.

Indexicality and deixis

The third class of referring expressions mentioned, though not discussed, in the previous section is that of pronouns. Traditionally, pronouns are thought of as noun-substitutes (as the term 'pronoun' suggests). But most subclasses of pronouns (other than relative pronouns: 'who', 'which' in English) also have a quite different function, which arguably is more basic than that of standing for an antecedent noun or noun-phrase. This is their *indexical* or *deictic* function. We have already met the terms 'indexicality' and 'deixis' in Chapter 9; and the term 'index' was used in a related sense, in our discussion of model-theoretic semantics, in Chapter 7. Indexicality and deixis will be dealt with from a much broader point of view in this section. The only subclasses of pronouns that will be mentioned are *personal* pronouns, on the one hand ('I', 'you', 'we', etc.), and *demonstrative* pronouns, on the other ('this', 'that'). But 'indexicality' and 'deixis' are commonly employed nowadays to cover a far wider range of phenomena, including demonstrative adverbs ('here', 'there'), tense (past, present and future), and such lexical differences as are exemplified in English by the verbs 'come' *vs* 'go' or 'bring' *vs* 'take'.

As far as I am aware, no one has drawn a systematic and theoretically well-motivated distinction between the terms 'indexicality' and 'deixis'. Both of them, as we shall see, can be explained, from an etymological point of view, on the basis of the notion of gestural reference. But they have entered linguistics and related disciplines by different routes. 'Indexicality' (or rather 'index' from which 'indexicality' derives) was introduced into logic and the philosophy of language by the American philosopher

C.S. Peirce (mentioned, in another connection, in Chapter 2); it is only recently that it has been employed by linguists. 'Deixis' (and more especially the adjective 'deictic') has a much longer, not to say nobler, pedigree – going back as it does to the work of the ancient Greek grammarians; but it was made familiar to linguists and others, in the sense that it now bears, by the German psychologist K. Bühler (1879–1963). It would be in the spirit of the use that is currently made of the two terms in philosophy, linguistics and psychology to think of indexicality as a particular kind of deixis: namely, as deixis insofar as it is relevant to the determination of the propositional meaning of utterances. I will tacitly adopt this view. However, I would emphasize that I am doing no more than codifying a historically explicable difference of usage. It so happens that the philosophical tradition in which 'indexicality' has been defined is one that takes a characteristically narrow view of meaning.

As I said earlier, the terms 'deixis' and 'index' both originate in the notion of *gestural reference*: that is, in the identification of the referent by means of some bodily gesture on the part of the speaker. ('Deixis' means "pointing" or "showing" in Greek; 'index' is the Latin word for the pointing-finger. Pointing is one, culturally established, method of identification by bodily gesture.) Any referring expression which has the same logical properties as a bodily gesture is, by virtue of that fact, deictic. Personal and demonstrative pronouns, in their relevant uses, are the most obvious kinds of linguistic expressions that have such properties, and they are clearly deictic in terms of this etymological definition. For example, instead of saying *I am happy* a speaker could point to himself and say *Happy*; instead of saying *That's beautiful*, he could point to a particular painting at an exhibition and say *Beautiful*. Of course, he could simultaneously point to the referent and use the appropriate deictic expression; and many deictic expressions are normally used, in fact, in association with some kind of gestural reference. It is worth noting at this point that the philosophical notion of *ostensive definition* (as was made clear, though not in these terms, in Chapter 3) rests upon an understanding of gestural reference and deixis. ('Ostension' is in any case simply a Latin-based word with the same meaning, etymologically speaking, as 'deixis'.)

Etymology may explain the source of the term 'deixis'; it cannot of course account fully for its current use. To do this we must invoke the notion of the deictic context, operating as an integral part of the context of utterance. Every act of utterance – every locutionary act – occurs in a spatio-temporal context whose centre, or zero-point, can be referred to as here-and-now. But how do we identify the here-and-now on particular occasions of utterance? A moment's reflection will convince us that there is no other way of defining the demonstrative adverbs 'here' and 'now' (or their equivalents in other languages) than by relating them to the place and time of utterance: 'here' refers to where the speaker is and 'now' refers to the moment of utterance (or some period of time that contains the moment of utterance). The complementary demonstrative adverbs 'there' and 'then' are negatively defined in relation to 'here' and 'now': 'there' means "not-here" and 'then' means "not-now".

The deictic context, then, is centred upon the speaker's here-and-now. It is characterized, in fact, by a particular kind of speaker-based egocentricity. The first-person pronoun, 'I' in English, refers (normally) to the speaker himself. As the role of speaker – more generally, the role of the locutionary agent – passes from one person to another in the course of a conversation, so the zero-point of the deictic context will be switched back and forth, together with the reference of 'I' and 'here'. The reference of 'now' does not, of course, switch back and forth in the same way, since speaker and hearer normally operate with the same temporal frame of reference and common assumptions about the passage of time: but 'now' is continuously redefined, within this shared temporal frame of reference, by the act of utterance. So, too, of course, are past, present and future, which are defined, explicitly or implicitly, in relation to the now of utterance. We can think of the pronoun 'I' and the demonstrative adverbs 'here' and 'now' – and of their equivalents in other languages – as referring expressions which single out and identify the logically separable components of the spatio-temporal zero-point of the deictic context. All three components (with or without others that will not be discussed here) are commonly included in the index, or point of reference, in model-theoretic semantics. And each such index, as we have seen, distinguishes one possible world from its alternatives.

I will not go into the details of spatio-temporal deixis. The way in which it can tell us what proposition has been expressed (in the utterance of a particular sentence by a particular speaker at a particular time) has been illustrated in Chapter 9. All that needs to be done here is to emphasize the general point that most utterance-inscriptions in all languages are indexical or deictic, in the sense that the truth-value of the propositions that they express is determined by the spatio-temporal dimensions of the deictic context. If the utterance-inscription contains a personal pronoun, a demonstrative of any kind, a verb in the past, present or future tense, any one of a whole host of expressions like 'yesterday', 'next year', 'abroad', or a verb like 'come' or 'bring', the fact that it will express different propositions in different deictic contexts is obvious enough.

But the spatio-temporal dimensions of the deictic context may be implicit in an utterance even when they are not made explicit either grammatically or lexically. Let us consider, for example, an utterance like

It is raining.

Unless there are contextual indications to the contrary (e.g., the speaker might be reporting the content of a long-distance telephone conversation), it will refer to the time and place of the act of utterance itself: it will be

logically equivalent to
> *It is raining here and now.*

English, of course, like many languages, grammaticalizes the temporal dimension of the deictic context in its tense-system. If we were to translate *It is raining* into a language without tense (e.g., Chinese or Malay), there would be no explicit indication in the utterance-inscription itself of the fact that it referred to the present, rather than to the past or the future: both "now" and "here" (and not only "here" as in English) would be implicit.

Languages vary enormously with respect to the degree to which they grammaticalize or lexicalize spatio-temporal deixis. It is also important to realize that even languages that are superficially very similar (e.g., English, French, German) may differ considerably in many points of detail. For example, French 'ici' and 'là' do not exactly match English 'here' and 'there'; German 'kommen' and 'bringen' do not exactly match 'come' and 'bring'. A good deal of research on spatio-temporal deixis has been carried out recently from several points of view, but so far on only a very limited number of the world's languages. The evidence currently available reinforces the view taken here: that its role in natural languages is all-pervasive. Theoretical semantics and pragmatics have made a start, as we have seen, with the problem of formalization; but there is still a long way to go.

Two distinctions must now be drawn. The first is between what I will call *pure* and *impure* deixis: between expressions whose meaning can be accounted for fully in terms of the notion of deixis and expressions whose meaning is partly deictic and partly non-deictic. For example, the first-person and second-person pronouns in English, 'I' and 'you', are purely deictic: they refer to the locutionary agent and the addressee without conveying any additional information about them. Similarly, the demonstratives, 'this' *vs* 'that' and 'here' *vs* 'there', when they are used with spatio-temporal reference, are pure deictics: they identify the referent (an entity or a place) in relation to the location of the locutionary act and its participants. The third-person singular pronouns, on the other hand, – 'he', 'she' and 'it' – are impure deictics: they encode the distinctions of meaning that are traditionally associated with the terms 'masculine', 'feminine' and 'neuter'. Since these distinctions are based upon properties of the referent which have nothing to do with his, her or its spatio-temporal location or role in the locutionary act, they are clearly non-deictic. Once again, languages vary considerably with respect to the kind of non-deictic information that they combine with deictic information in the meaning of particular expressions. For example, in many languages gender is not based upon the sex of the referent or its sortal categorization as human, animal or inanimate, but on its shape, size, texture or edibility.

It is also important to note that the non-deictic part of the meaning of impure deictics may be descriptive (or propositional), social or expressive. For example, when 'she' is used, meaning "the female person", to refer to a girl or a woman, the non-deictic part of its meaning is descriptive. But when it is used, typically by a man, to refer to his car or a piece of machinery, it is expressive – though what attitude it expresses (and whether it is rightly called sexist) is matter for dispute! As for social meaning, this is very commonly encoded in the meaning of pronouns: notably, and on a scale that is unparalleled in European languages, in Japanese, Korean, Javanese and many languages of South-East Asia. The so-called T/V distinction that is found in many European languages – 'tu' *vs* 'vous' in French, 'du' *vs* 'Sie' in German, 'tu' *vs* 'usted' in Spanish, etc. – which has been much discussed recently in the sociolinguistic and psycholinguistic literature, exemplifies the phenomenon on a relatively small scale and in respect only of the pronouns used to refer to the addressee. In all the languages that have the T/V distinction, the non-deictic meaning that is associated with it is primarily social, being determined by social role or the relatively stable interpersonal relations that hold between speaker and addressee. But in some languages (e.g., Russian), the switch from the T-pronoun to the V-pronoun, or conversely, can also indicate the speaker's change of mood or attitude. This is but one example, however, of the tendency for social and expressive meaning to merge and to be, at times, inseparable.

The second distinction (which is not to be confused with the distinction between pure and impure deixis) is between *primary* and *secondary* deixis. Primary deixis is of the kind that can be accounted for in terms of gestural reference within the framework of the deictic context as this has been described above. Secondary deixis involves the displacement or re-interpretation of the spatio-temporal dimensions of the primary deictic context. This displacement or re-interpretation can be of several different kinds, and in some cases it can be appropriately called metaphorical. Here, I will give just one example.

As primary deictics, the English demonstratives can be analysed in terms of the notion of spatio-temporal proximity to the deictic centre: 'this' and 'here' refer to entities and places that are located in the place that contains the speaker (or to points or periods of time that are located in the period of time that contains the moment of utterance) – this is what 'proximity' means when it is used, technically, in discussions of deixis. Of course, the boundaries of the place or time that contains the deictic centre can be shifted indefinitely far from the centre: 'here' can have the same reference as 'this room' or 'this galaxy', and 'now' the same reference as 'this moment' or 'this year'. There are complications of detail (and arguably the traditional term 'proximity' is misleading). But the principle is clear, insofar as it is relevant to the present example. Now, among the several uses of the demonstratives that can be analysed in terms of the notion of secondary deixis, there is a particular use of 'that' *vs* 'this' which is recognizably expressive, and whose expressivity can be identified as that of emotional or attitudinal dissociation. For example, if a speaker is holding something in the hand he will normally use 'this', rather than 'that', to refer to it (by virtue of its spatio-temporal proximity). If he says *What's that?* in such circumstances, his use of 'that' will be indicative of his dislike or aversion: he will be distancing himself emotionally or attitudinally from whatever he is referring to.

This is but one example of one kind of secondary deixis. I have chosen it because it illustrates fairly clearly (and without the need for long preliminary explanation of unfamiliar linguistic material or additional technical distinctions) what I mean by the displacement or re-interpretation of a primarily spatio-temporal dimension of the deictic context. There is at least an intuitively evident connection between physical and emotional proximity or remoteness.

As we shall see in the next section, secondary deixis of the kind that has been illustrated here is very close to subjective modality. Before turning to that and related topics, however, I should make it clear that the distinction that I have drawn here between primary and secondary deixis rests upon the conventional view according to which deixis is to be defined, first and foremost, as a matter of spatio-temporal location in the context of utterance. An alternative, and perhaps defensible, view is that the egocentricity of the deictic context is of its very nature subjective – in the sense in which 'subjectivity' will be explained in the following section.

Modality, subjectivity and locutionary agency

In this final section of the book I want to bring together, summarily and rather dogmatically, three notions that have not been related as closely as they ought to have been in most recent work in semantics and pragmatics: modality, subjectivity and locutionary agency. In fact, it is probably true to say that, as far as works written in English are concerned, the vast majority of them are seriously flawed, from a theoretical point of view, by their failure to give due weight to these three notions and their interdependence. This failure is perhaps attributable to the empiricist tradition, which still weighs heavily on mainstream British and American philosophy, psychology, sociology and, to a lesser extent, linguistics. The reassertion of Cartesian rationalism, by Chomsky and others, in recent years has done nothing to remedy the defects of empiricism in this respect. For British empiricism and Cartesian rationalism (in the form in which it has been taken over and reinterpreted) both share the intellectualist prejudice that language is essentially an instrument for the expression of propositional thought. This prejudice is evident in a large number of influential works, which, though they might differ considerably on a wide variety of issues, are at one in giving no attention at all to the non-propositional component of languages or in playing down its importance. The same prejudice is evident in standard logical treatments of modality.

The only kind of *modality* recognized in traditional modal logic is that which has to do with the notions of necessity and possibility insofar as they relate to the truth (and falsity) of propositions: *Aletheutic* modality ('aletheutic' comes from the Greek word for truth). We have already looked at the question of the necessary truth and falsity of propositions on several occasions, and with particular reference to entailment and analyticity in Chapter 4. In Chapter 6, we noted that the modal operators N and M, like the operator of negation in the propositional calculus, are truth-functional. At this point, it may be added that aletheutic necessity and possibility are interdefinable under negation. To take the example used in Chapter 6: "Necessarily, the sky is blue" is logically equivalent to "It is not possible that the sky is not blue" ($Np \Leftrightarrow \sim M \sim p$); and "Possibly, the sky is blue" is logically equivalent to "It is not necessarily the case that the sky is not blue" (($Mp \Leftrightarrow \sim N \sim p$). There are other kinds of necessity and possibility that have the same logical properties with respect to negation.

Aletheutic modality, then, like propositional negation, is by definition truth-functional. But what about modality in the everyday use of natural languages? Let us take another of the examples used in Chapter 6: the sentence 'He may not come'. Now, there is no doubt that this sentence can be used to assert a modalized negative proposition (with either external or internal negation: either $\sim Mp$ or $M \sim p$). In this case both the negative particle *not* and the modal verb 'may' are construed objectively: as contributing to the propositional content of the sentence.

But with this particular sentence, the modality is more likely to be either *epistemic* or *deontic* than aletheutic. The terms 'epistemic' and 'deontic' were introduced, it will be recalled, in Chapter 8: I will now employ them, without formal definition, as they are used in modern modal logic. If our sample sentence is given an *objective* epistemic interpretation, its propositional content will be "Relative to what is known, it is possible that he will not come"; if it is given an *objective* deontic interpretation, its propositional content will be "It is not permitted that he come". In both cases, it will be noted, the modality is represented as something that holds, as a matter of fact, in some epistemic or deontic world which is external to whoever utters the sentence on particular occasions of utterance. This is what I mean by the objectification of modality.

However, independently of whether the sentence 'He may not come' is construed epistemically or deontically, the modality associated with 'may' can be *subjective*, rather than objective: that is to say, in uttering this sentence, a locutionary agent can be expressing his own beliefs and attitudes, rather than reporting, as a neutral observer, the existence of this or that state of affairs. Subjective modality is much more common than objective modality in most everyday uses of language; and objective epistemic modality, in particular, is very rare. If 'He may not come' is uttered with subjective epistemic modality, it means something like "I-think-it-possible that he will not come" (where the hyphenated "I-think-it-possible" is to be taken as a unit); if it is uttered with subjective deontic modality, it means something like "I forbid him to come".

The terms 'epistemic' and 'deontic' were used in Chapter 8 in connection with the notion of illocutionary commitment. At that point I talked as if the only options open to the locutionary agent were those of full commitment and the withholding of commitment. We now see that this is not so. As far as making statements is concerned, there are various ways in which a locutionary agent can qualify his epistemic commitment. He can indicate that his evidence for what he asserts is less good than it might be; that his commitment is tentative, provisional or conditional, rather than absolute; and so on. Subjective epistemic modality is nothing other than this: the locutionary agent's qualification of his epistemic commitment. All natural spoken languages provide their users with the prosodic resources – stress and intonation – with which to express these several distinguishable kinds of qualified epistemic commitment. Some, but by no means all, grammaticalize them in the category of mood; and some languages, like English, lexicalize or semi-lexicalize them by means of modal verbs ('may', 'must', etc.), modal adjectives ('possible', etc.), modal adverbs ('possibly', etc.) and modal particles ('perhaps', etc.).

Assertion, in the technical sense of the term, implies full unqualified epistemic commitment. Relatively few of our everyday statements have this neutral, dispassionate, totally non-subjective character. English, however, does allow us to make statements which can be reasonably classified as assertions. It also allows us, as we have seen, to objectify both epistemic and deontic modality – by propositionalizing the content of modal verbs or adverbs and bringing this within the scope of the illocutionary agent's unqualified "I say so". But English is certainly not typical of the world's languages in this respect. It may well be true, as we assumed in Chapter 8, that all languages enable their users to make statements of one kind or another; it is not the case that all natural languages provide their users with the means of making modally unqualified assertions. For example, there are many American Indian languages that have several non-indicative moods, for different kinds of epistemic modality, but no indicative mood. (Apart from anything else, this fact reinforces the points made in Chapter 6, about the necessity of distinguishing 'declarative' from 'indicative'.)

It is also worth drawing attention to the fact that it is often difficult to draw a sharp distinction, from a semantic or pragmatic point of view, between tense and mood. Even in English, where tense can be identified without much difficulty as a deictic category, there are uses of what are traditionally described as the past, present and future tenses that have more to do with the expression of subjective modality than with primary deixis. For example, when he says *That will be the postman*, the speaker is more likely to be making an epistemically qualified statement about the present than an unqualified assertion about the future; when he says *I wanted to ask you whether you needed the car today*, he is more likely to be making a tentative or hesitant request than to be describing some past state of consciousness. Some of these modal uses of the tenses could perhaps be accounted for in terms of the notion of secondary deixis. But, as I mentioned in the previous section, secondary deixis and subjective modality are often indistinguishable. Although I shall not go into the question in this book, I should also mention that, looked at from a more general point of view, tense itself can be seen as being primarily a matter of modality.

It now remains to make explicit, not simply in relation to modality but more generally, the sense in which I am using the term 'subjectivity' in this section. When I talk about the *subjectivity of utterance*, I am referring to the locutionary agent's expression of himself in the act of utterance and of the reflection of this in the phonological, grammatical and lexical structure of the utterance-inscription. Two points need to be emphasized in connection with the notion of self-expression to which I am appealing in this definition of 'subjectivity'.

First, I want the term 'self-expression' to be taken literally. The self is not to be understood as being logically and psychologically distinguishable from the beliefs, attitudes and emotions of which it is the seat or location. Still less is it to be taken, as it commonly is in the dominant intellectualist tradition referred to at the beginning of this section, as the reasoning faculty operating dispassionately upon the propositions stored in the mind or brought to it for judgment from observation of the external world. Throughout this book, and especially in Part 4, I have been stressing the importance of the non-propositional aspect of language. The inadequacy of truth-conditional semantics as a total theory, not only of utterance-meaning, but also of sentence-meaning, derives ultimately from its restriction to propositional content and its inability to handle the phenomenon of subjectivity. Self-expression cannot be reduced to the expression of propositional knowledge and beliefs.

Second, the self which the locutionary agent expresses is the product of the social and interpersonal roles that he has played in the past, and it manifests itself, in a socially identifiable way, in the role that he is playing in the context of utterance. As I pointed out in the discussion of Austin's theory of speech acts in Chapter 8, the central concepts of epistemic and deontic authority have a social basis. But they are vested by society in the individual; they are part of the self that he expresses whenever he utters a sentence in some socially appropriate context.

The subjectivity of utterance has not been much discussed, at least in the terms in which I have explained it here, in recent work in English. More attention has been devoted to it by French and German scholars, possibly because the notion of subjectivity itself plays a more important part in the Continental philosophical tradition. However that may be, it is my contention that there is much in the structure of all languages that cannot be explained without appealing to it; and also – though this is more debatable – that, for historical and ultimately social reasons, some languages are more deeply imbued with subjectivity than others.

At the end of Chapter 7, I mentioned the notion of accessibility between possible worlds. I said that a speaker must necessarily refer to the world that he is describing from the viewpoint of the world that he is in. I might just as well have put it the other way round, saying that a speaker must refer to the actual or non-actual world that he is describing from the viewpoint of the world that is in him. But, whichever way these relations of accessibility are formulated, it will now be clear that they can be explicated in terms of the account that has been given here of indexicality and subjective epistemic modality.

There is no reason to believe that these notions are beyond the scope of formalization. Indeed, my reference to the notion of accessibility, at the end of Chapter 7 and again at this point, is intended to suggest that model-theoretic, or indexical, semantics is not necessarily restricted to the truth-conditional part of linguistic meaning. It could doubtless be extended, to cover everything that has been discussed in this chapter as part of the subjectivity of utterance. Of course, there are those who might prefer to refer to any such extension as pragmatics, rather than semantics. But that is neither here nor there. As we have seen on several occasions, there are many different ways of drawing these terminological distinctions.

Summary

In this final chapter, I have dealt with three topics that everyone would agree are crucial in the construction of a theory of natural-language meaning: reference, deixis and modality. But I have done so, deliberately, from a rather unconventional viewpoint: I have given particular emphasis to what I have called the subjectivity of utterance. The terms 'subjectivity' and 'subjectivism' have rather a bad name in the social sciences. It is my conviction, however, that any theory of meaning which fails to account for the subjectivity of reference, deixis and modality, in the sense in which 'subjectivity' has been explained in this chapter, is condemned to sterility. As I have indicated here, there seems to be no reason in principle why this notion of subjectivity cannot be formalized.

Bibliography

The Bibliography lists all the works to which reference is made in the text, together with those mentioned in the Suggestions for Further Reading. I have also included a number of others whose content will usually be clear from their titles.

Allwood, J., Anderson, L.-G. & Dahl, Ö. (1977). *Logic in Linguistics*. Cambridge: Cambridge University Press.

Austin, J.L. (1962). *How To Do Things With Words*. Oxford: Clarendon Press.

Ayer, A.J. (1946). *Language, Truth and Logic*, 2nd edition. Gollancz: London.

Bar-Hillel, Y. (1970). *Aspects of Language*. Jerusalem: Magnes.

Bar-Hillel, Y. (ed.) (1971). *Pragmatics of Natural Language*. Dordrecht-Holland: Reidel.

Berlin, B. & Kay, P. (1969). *Basic Color Terms*. Berkeley & Los Angeles: University of California Press.

Bierwisch, M. (1970). 'Semantics'. In Lyons (1970: 166–84).

Bierwisch, M. (1971). 'On classifying semantic features' in Steinberg & Jakobovits (1971: 410–35).

Bloomfield, L. (1935). *Language*. London: Allen & Unwin. (American edition, 1933.)

Carnap, R. (1956). *Meaning and Necessity*, 2nd edition. Chicago: Chicago University Press.

Caton, C.E. (ed.) (1963). *Philosophy and Ordinary Language*. Urbana, Ill.: University of Illinois Press.

Chomsky, N. (1957). *Syntactic Structures*. The Hague: Mouton.

Chomsky, N. (1965). *Aspects of the Theory of Syntax*. Cambridge, Mass.: MIT Press.

Chomsky, N. (1972). *Studies on Semantics in Generative Grammar*. The Hague: Mouton.

Chomsky, N. (1977). *Essays in Form and Interpretation*. Amsterdam: North Holland.

Cole, P. & Morgan, J.L. (eds.) (1975). *Syntax and Semantics, 3*: *Speech Acts*. New York & London: Academic Press.

Collins Dictionary of the English Language, ed. Patrick Hanks (1979). London & Glasgow: Collins.

Dillon, G. (1977). *An Introduction to Contemporary Linguistic Semantics*. Englewood Cliffs, NJ: Prentice-Hall.

Dowty, D.R., Wall, R.E. & Peters, S. (1981). *Introduction to Montague Semantics*. Dordrecht-Holland, Boston & London: Reidel.

Dummett, M. (1973). *Frege: Philosophy of Language*. London: Duckworth.

Evans, G. & McDowell, J. (eds.) (1976). *Meaning and Truth*. London: Oxford University Press.

Feigl, H. & Sellars, W. (eds.) (1949). *Readings in Philosophical Analysis*. New York: Appleton-Century-Crofts.

Fillmore, C.J. (1966). 'Deictic categories in the semantics of "come" '. *Foundations of Language* 2. 219–27.

Fillmore, C.J. (1970). 'Subjects, speakers and roles'. *Synthese* 21. 251–74. (Reprinted in Davidson & Harman, 1972: 1–24.)

Fillmore, C.J. & Langendoen, D.T. (eds.) (1971). *Studies in Linguistic Semantics*. New York: Holt.

Fodor, J.A. & Katz, J.J. (1964). *The Structure of Language*: *Readings in the Philosophy of Language*. Englewood Cliffs, N.J.: Prentice-Hall.

Fodor, J.D. (1977). *Semantics: Theories of Meaning in Generative Linguistics*. New York: Crowell; Hassocks, Sussex: Harvester.

Fries, C.C. (1952). *The Structure of English*. New York: Harcourt Brace. (British edition, London: Longmans, 1957.)

Geach, P. & Black, M. (eds.) (1960). *Translations from the Philosophical Writings of Gottlob Frege*. Oxford: Blackwell.

Grice, H.P. (1975). 'Logic and conversation'. In Cole & Morgan (1975: 41–58).

Harman, G. & Davidson, D. (eds.) (1972). *Semantics of Natural Language*. Dordrecht-Holland: Reidel.

Hudson, R.A. (1980). *Sociolinguistics*. Cambridge: Cambridge University Press.

Hymes, D. (ed.) (1964). *Language in Culture and Society*. New York: Harper & Row.

Jacobs, R. & Rosenbaum, P.S. (eds.) (1970). *Readings in English Transformational Grammar*. Waltham, Mass.: Ginn.

Katz, J.J. (1972). *Semantic Theory*. New York: Harper & Row.

Katz, J.J. (1977). *Propositional Structure and Illocutionary Force*. New York: Crowell; Hassocks, Sussex: Harvester.

Katz, J.J. & Fodor, J.A. (1963). 'The structure of a semantic theory'. *Language* 39. 170–210. (Reprinted in Fodor & Katz, 1964: 479–518.)

Katz, J.J. & Postal, P.M. (1964). *An Integrated Theory of Linguistic Descriptions*. Cambridge, Mass.: MIT Press.

Keenan, E.L. (ed.) (1975). *Formal Semantics of Natural Language*. London & New York: Cambridge University Press.

Kempson, R.M. (1977). *Semantic Theory*. London, New York & Melbourne: Cambridge University Press.

Kooij, J.G. (1971). *Ambiguity in Natural Language*. Amsterdam. North-Holland.

Kripke, S. (1972) 'Naming and necessity'. In Harman & Davidson (1972: 253–355).

Leech, G.N. (1974). *Semantics*. Harmondsworth: Penguin.

Lehrer, A. (1974). *Semantic Fields and Lexical Structure*. Amsterdam & London: North-Holland.

Lehrer, K. & Lehrer, A. (eds.) (1970). *Theory of Meaning*. New York: Prentice-Hall.

Levinson, S. (1981). *Pragmatics*. Cambridge: Cambridge University Press.

Linsky, L. (ed.) (1971). *Reference and Modality*. London: Oxford University Press.

Longman Dictionary of Contemporary English (1978). London: Longman.

Lyons, J. (ed.) (1970). *New Horizons in Linguistics*. Harmondsworth: Penguin Books.

Lyons, J. (1977a). *Chomsky*, 2nd edition. London: Fontana; New York: Viking/Penguin. (1st edition, 1970.)

Lyons, J. (1977b). *Semantics*, 2 vols. London & New York: Cambridge University Press.

Lyons, J. (1981). *Language and Linguistics*. Cambridge, New York & Melbourne: Cambridge University Press.

McCawley, J.D. (1981). *Everything that Linguists have Always Wanted to Know about Logic* (1981). Chicago, New York & London: University of Chicago Press.

Montague, R. (1974). *Formal Philosophy: Selected Papers of Richard Montague*, edited with an introduction by Richmond Thomason. New Haven, Conn.: Yale University Press.

Morris, C.W. (1938). 'Foundations of the theory of signs'. In Neurath, Carnap & Morris (1938: 79–137).

Morris, C.W. (1946). *Signs, Language and Behaviour*. New York: Prentice-Hall.

Neurath, O., Carnap, R. & Morris, C.W. (eds.) (1938). *International Encyclopaedia of Unified Sciences*. (Combined edition 1955.) Chicago: University of Chicago Press.

Nida, E. (1975). *Componential Analysis of Meaning*. The Hague: Mouton.

Ogden, C.K. (1968). *Basic English: International Second Language*. (Revised and expanded edition of *The System of Basic English*.) New York: Harcourt Brace.

Olshewsky, T.M. (ed.) (1969). *Problems in the Philosophy of Language*. New York: Holt, Rinehart & Winston.

Palmer, F.R. (1979). *Modality and the English Modals*. London: Longman.

Palmer, F.R. (1981). *Semantics: A New Outline*, 2nd edition. Cambridge: Cambridge University Press. (1st edition, 1976.)

Parkinson, G. (ed.) (1968). *The Theory of Meaning*. London: Oxford University Press.

Partee, B.H. (1975). 'Montague grammar and transformational grammar'. *Linguistic Inquiry* 6. 203–300.

Peirce, C.S. (1940). *The Philosophy of Peirce: Selected Writings*, edited by J. Buchler. London: Kegan Paul.

Popper, K. (1963). *Conjectures and Refutations*. London: Routledge & Kegan Paul.

Putnam, H. (1970). 'Is semantics possible?'. In H. Kiefer & M. Munitz (eds.) *Languages, Belief and Metaphysics*. New York: State University of New York Press, 1970. (Reprinted in Putnam, 1975: 139–52.)

Putnam, H. (1975). *Mind, Language and Reality*. London & New York: Cambridge University Press.

Quine, W.V. (1953). *From a Logical Point of View*. Cambridge, Mass.: Harvard University Press.

Quine, W.V. (1960). *Word and Object*. Cambridge, Mass.: MIT Press.

Reichenbach, H. (1947) *Elements of Symbolic Logic*. London & New York: Macmillan.

Roget, P.M. (1852). *Thesaurus of English Words and Phrases*. London. (Abridged and revised, London: Penguin, 1953.)

Rosenberg, J. & Travis, C. (eds.) (1971). *Readings in the Philosophy of Language*. New York: Prentice-Hall.

Russell, B. (1940). *An Inquiry into Meaning and Truth*. London: Allen & Unwin. (Reprinted Harmondsworth, Middlesex: Penguin Books, 1962.)

Ryle, G. (1951). 'The theory of meaning'. In Mace, C.A. (ed.) *British Philosophy in the Mid-Century*. London: Allen & Unwin, 239–64. (Reprinted in Zabeeh *et al.* 1974: 219–44.)

Sapir, E. (1949). *Selected Writings in Language, Culture and Personality*, edited by D.G. Mandelbaum, Berkeley: University of California Press.

Searle, J.R. (1969). *Speech Acts*. London & New York: Cambridge University Press.

Smith, N.V. & Wilson, D. (1979). *Modern Linguistics: The Results of the Chomskyan Revolution*. Harmondsworth: Penguin.

Steinberg, D.D. & Jakobovits, L.A. (eds.) (1971). *Semantics*. London & New York: Cambridge University Press.

Strawson, P.F. (1971). *Logico-Linguistic Papers*. London: Methuen.

Tarski, A. (1944). 'The semantic conception of truth'. *Philosophy and Phenomenological Research* 4. 341–75. (Reprinted in Tarski, 1956; Olshewsky, 1969; Zabeeh *et al.*, 1974.)

Tarski, A. (1956). *Logic, Semantics, Metamathematics*. London: Oxford University Press.

Ullmann, S. (1962). *Semantics*. Oxford: Blackwell; New York: Barnes & Noble.

Waldron, R.A. (1979). *Sense and Sense Development*, 2nd edition. London: Deutsch. (1st edition, 1967.)

Whorf, B.L. (1956). *Language, Thought and Reality: Selected Writings of Benjamin Lee Whorf*, edited by J.B. Carroll. New York: Wiley.

Wittgenstein, L. (1953). *Philosophical Investigations*. Oxford: Blackwell; New York: Macmillan.

Zabeeh, F., Klemke, E.D. & Jacobson, A. (eds.) (1974). *Readings in Semantics*. Urbana, Chicago & London: University of Illinois Press.

Suggestions for Further Reading

Almost everything dealt with in this book is treated in greater detail, and with full supporting bibliography in Lyons (1977b), to which the present work will serve as an introduction. Less comprehensive recently published books on semantics, representative of various points of view, include Dillon (1977), Leech (1974), Palmer (1981), Waldron (1979) and, at a rather more advanced level, Kempson (1977). Ullman (1962) is still useful as an introduction to lexical semantics.

Readers with no previous background in linguistics may find it helpful to consult Lyons (1981): this contains a simplified exposition of linguistic semantics (in Chapter 5) which is conceptually and terminologically compatible with the one given here and sets linguistic semantics within a more general historical and theoretical framework. It also provides guidance on reading in many relevant areas of linguistics and explains some of the differences between one school and another.

Much of what I classify as semantics (in accordance with the more traditional view) is nowadays treated by linguists and philosophers as a part of pragmatics or sociolinguistics: cf. Levinson (1981) and Hudson (1980), for full accounts of recent work. Many classic articles from an earlier period are reprinted in Hymes (1974).

For the philosophical background, reference may be made to one or more of the following: Caton (1963), Lehrer & Lehrer (1970), Olshewsky (1969), Parkinson (1968), Rosenberg & Travis (1971), Zabeeh *et al.* (1974). As to formal logic: Allwood *et al.* (1977) is to be recommended and, for a broader and more personal view, McCawley (1981).

Index